California Friendly®

A maintenance guide for
landscapers, gardeners and
land managers

Douglas Kent

CALIFORNIA FRIENDLY®: A MAINTENANCE GUIDE FOR LANDSCAPERS, GARDENERS AND LAND MANAGERS

1ST EDITION MARCH 2017

Published by: Douglas Kent + Associates
164 S. Pixley St.
Orange, CA 92868
www.anfractus.com

Author: Douglas Kent
Editor: Sharon Cohoon
Executive Editors/Producers
      Melisa Marks Southern California Gas Company
      Craig Tranby Los Angeles Department of Water and Power
      Bill McDonnell Metropolitan Water District of Southern California
Technical Editors: Ellen Mackey, Mark A. Daniel, Carlos Gavina, Mark Gentili, Susanne Kluh, Jevon Lam, Madalyn Le, Cathleen Chavez-Morris, Enrique Silva, Maria Sison-Roces, Anthony Tew and Matthew Veeh
Illustrations and Photos: Douglas Kent, unless noted in caption
Layout and Book Design: Hilal Sala Productions
Front and Back Cover Design: Christina Holland and the Public Relations Team at the Los Angeles Department of Water and Power
Photo Editor: Debbie Dunne
Special Assistance: Jaana Nieuwboer

ISBN: 978-0-692-80026-3
Created and produced in Southern California

Dedication

This book is dedicated to the all the people caring for California's landscapes. It is for the people planting and pruning our gardens, raking and sweeping our surfaces, and monitoring and adjusting our irrigation systems (conserving our precious water). Creating and maintaining landscapes takes all kinds of people: owners, managers, contractors, vendors and specialists are vital to a landscape's success. But it is the men and women in our gardens that ultimately get the job done—the people who get their hands dirty hauling manure, scrape their skin reaching for a weed, and endure harsh weather to preserve beautiful spaces. This sturdy group of professionals maintains the sustainable vision of our communities, and ultimately, our health.

We hope this book will be like a good hand pruner or shovel for you, another tool to make your work easier and more successful.

Contents

PART I
Introduction

1

Your Water and Energy— let's get this right!

California Friendly® landscaping isn't about plant lists, although it includes them. It isn't about irrigation guidelines, although those are provided as well. What California Friendly® landscaping is about is long-term sustainability, resiliency, and livability. It *is* about landscaping that is friendly to all Californians, both now and well into the future.

The California Friendly® Landscaping program was designed to inspire a style appropriate for our semi-arid climate and this more sustainable style is catching on. Between the years 2008 and 2016 Southern Californians ripped out over 167 million square feet of turf and replaced it with plants that are well adapted to our climate. Our region has made a big investment in California Friendly® landscapes. Now our challenge is to maintain them.

Regrettably, many people struggle to maintain resource-conserving landscapes. They believe that resource-conserving means zero-maintenance which, of course, is not true. The consequences have been as bad for property managers as they have been for the conservation movement. Poor maintenance has created visually unappealing and ecologically ineffective landscapes—and all of this creates a reason for people to migrate back to their water wasting ways.

California Friendly® landscapes call for a new attitude towards maintenance. It is one that requires more engagement, examination and acceptance.

Engage with your soil. Bend down and get personally acquainted. Nothing improves irrigation efficiency and plant health more than someone willing to dig in and become familiar with the soil. Smelling earth provides cues to its levels of organic matter and oxygen. Letting it crumble and fall through your fingers tells you about the amount of biological activity it contains. And digging down several inches teaches you there is often more moisture in the soil than is evident on the surface. All of this information is important, and all of it is gained by getting closer to the soil.

Examine the rest of the landscape. Getting to know weeds helps you identify soil conditions. Looking at leaves to identify potential problems helps you fine tune irrigation and fertilization schedules. And becoming familiar with bugs, funguses, and other pests provides cues for pruning and planting. Signs are everywhere. We just need to take the time to look for them.

Accept that a more natural landscape is going to be a little wilder. It may have a few more weeds and bugs, but with them come more connections to nature and more long-term security. We also need to accept that plants and soil dictate irrigation, pruning, and planting schedules, not a calendar.

The purpose of this book is to help you maintain a California Friendly® Landscape. With it you can:

- Maintain irrigation efficiency through time and change.
- Maintain aesthetic qualities through time and change.
- Maintain a landscape's ability to slow, stop and clean stormwater runoff.

Take this book into the field with you and dig in. It will absolutely help. From irrigation and fertilization, to mulches and infiltration areas, this book provides a solid foundation. But no matter how good a manual is, it is only a book. California Friendly® landscapes are maintained by people. Designers and gardeners, budget directors and advocates, we all have a hand in a landscape's success. We all have a hand in Southern California's health. Let's get dirty.

See you in the garden,

Doug

It's Just Not Water

Landscapes are essential to the long-term survivability of Southern California. They provide incredible benefits. Landscapes positively impact economic welfare, public health, and ecological wellbeing. They protect aquatic environments, clean the air, and provide a wealth of recreational opportunities. We need them.

But landscaping has costs, too. Some of these costs are enormous. We use pesticides that kill not just the targeted pest but all insects, including the beneficial ones. We spread chemical fertilizers across great expanses, allowing the nutrients to slowly seep or run off, diminishing watery ecosystems. And we lavish our landscapes with water, and all of its embodied energy.

Energy is embedded into every drop of water we use. From extraction, transportation and treatment, to distribution and the handling of wastewater, every step is energy-drenched. A majority of the water in California is moved with either natural gas pumps or electrical pumps. About 30% of that total pump power comes from natural gas.

While the use of renewable gas and electric energies will continue to grow, they are currently variable in supply. Solar only works in the day and wind turbines only when it is windy. To get through these periods of low or no generation we'll need efficient energy storage and reduced energy use during off-generation hours.

California Friendly® Landscaping can meet, if not exceed, the state's goals for carbon reduction and water and energy conservation, and still provide immense benefit. These landscapes can sequester up to 300% more carbon than is released through irrigation; they can reduce residential cooling costs by as much as 50%, and they can infiltrate 80% of a rain event onsite—all for minimal water and energy costs.

California Friendly® landscapes are a good investment, for all of us.

PART II

Irrigation: Maintaining Efficiency

The Gist of Irrigation

Landscape irrigation is a luxury. Urban areas in Southern California can exist without it by using fewer plants and only varieties that could exist entirely on rainfall. But our quality of life would suffer as a result. A rich varied landscape enriches our urban experience in numerous ways.

Landscapes have a profound impact. They improve public health. Air quality, emotional wellbeing and longevity are all affected by landscapes. They provide many services, such as urban cooling, holding soils, and providing food. And their inherent beauty increases property values and helps spur community pride and engagement.

All these benefits are reasons why we irrigate. However, we can no longer continue to do it in the same unmindful way we have in the past. Water has become too precious for that. Modern realities mandate that we use every drop wisely.

Using water wisely, however, is not a straightforward task. The picture below illustrates the inherent problem. During the drought years, the sprinklers in this area were turned down. That worked for some areas, but obviously not for others. Increasing the irrigation frequency and duration would have greened up the brown areas, but doing so would have overwatered the areas that were already green. The problem illustrated here, unfortunately, applies to nearly all irrigation systems; one value will underwater some areas, overwater others, and be perfectly suited to still others.

Irrigation is inherently inefficient. One value will almost always underwater some areas, overwater others, and be perfectly suited to still others.

The goal of the Irrigation sections of this book is to reduce the scale and size of this problem. This first chapter provides an overview of irrigation. The second chapter explains how to program an irrigation controller/timer for maximum efficiency. The third irrigation chapter highlights maintenance practices, timing of tasks, and troubleshooting common problems. The fourth, and last chapter, explains how to get the most from irrigating with recycled water.

Types of Systems

For the purposes of this book there are only two types of irrigation systems: high-pressure and low-pressure. Each has advantages and disadvantages.

High-Pressure

Designed to distribute water over a large area in a short period of time, high-pressure systems use rotor heads, impact spray heads, regular spray heads and bubblers.

Advantages

- One sprinkler head can cover hundreds if not thousands of square feet and costs per sq. ft. of wetted surface are low.

- Because of the expansive coverage, maintenance costs are low.

- Installation and maintenance can be managed by a layperson, although efficiency usually suffers.

Disadvantages

- These systems are terribly water wasting—up to 50% of a sprinklers water can be lost to evaporation and wind drift.

- Water costs are higher than low-pressure systems.

- Improper use of system can lead to many kinds of infestations: fungus, insects, molds and weeds.

- Overspray from sprinklers contributes to dry-season runoff and the deterioration of our stream and ocean environments.

Low-Pressure

Designed to reduce inefficiencies and water loss, low-pressure irrigation delivers water directly to where the plant needs it, with little or no evaporation, overspray and runoff. There are three broad categories: drip (micro-sprayers, bubblers, emitters), inline emitter tubing, and soaker hose.

Advantages

■ These systems can be precise and deliver water only where the plant needs it.

■ The systems can be very water conserving.

■ Water costs are lower than high-pressure.

Disadvantages

■ Both the installation and maintenance costs are higher.

■ Tubing breaks down in sun.

■ Easily disrupted by people and pets.

■ Prone to blockage with hard water.

■ Can be chewed through by animals.

■ If not used properly, it can cause salts to accumulate.

■ While anyone can design, install and maintain a system, they generally work better when professionally done.

What is Good Irrigation?

A well functioning irrigation system will go on when a soil dries to a predetermined depth and then replenish the moisture lost. It will neither irrigate before the plants need it, nor deliver water deeper than the plants need it. There is also no overspray or runoff.

The most important part of an efficient irrigation system is the observer. A careful irrigator must look at the system, the soil and the plants in order to identify irrigation and water problems. Below are the methods used to gauge soil moisture and the characteristics of landscapes that are either too wet or too dry.

Irrigation Communities

The plants listed in this book are drought-adapted and drought-tolerant, but that does not mean that they evolved without moisture. Nearly every plant has a period of growth and a natural period of dormancy. The challenge is to ensure proper moisture when they are growing (water need) and reducing moisture when they are not (water waste). The California Friendly plant palette has three broad types of irrigation communities:

- Coastal Influenced: Many of our coastal natives start growing with the start of the rainy season, in late October, early November. Success with these plants is achieved by ensuring proper levels of moisture November through March. As the seasons progress moisture levels should taper off encouraging natural dormancy by late summer.

- Freeze Influenced: Plants native to the colder regions start growing after the last frost, typically late February/early March. Success with this group is achieved by maintaining just enough moisture late February through June and then reducing levels of moisture as summer moves into fall.

- Monsoon Influenced: Many desert natives evolved to moisture twice a year: winter and summer. Success with this group comes from maintaining just enough moisture during these two primary growing seasons. Moisture levels can dramatically fall in spring and fall.

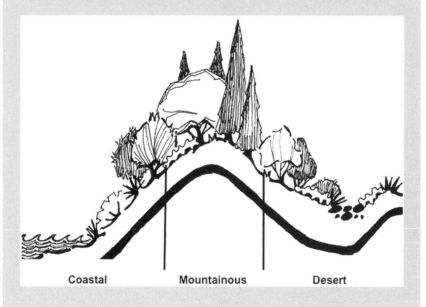

Coastal   Mountainous   Desert

Gauging Soil Moisture

Soil testing is essential to irrigation efficiency. Below are the most common methods of physically testing soil moisture.

■ **Coring:** Whether using a soil sampling device or simply a metal pipe and hammer, this method pulls up a ½" sample at depths of up to 2 feet. This is the most accurate method of measurement because it engages sight, smell and touch.

■ **Dig:** A quick method when dry-to depth is between 2" and 5"; after that, it is not so quick. It is also the most intrusive and damaging method.

■ **Dowel:** Pushing or driving a dowel into the soil and letting it remain for a minute or so provides an accurate picture of moisture levels. Dowels readily absorb available water. They will also pick up a soil's scent.

■ **Electronics:** Soil probes typically measure electrical conductivity and not actual water volume. This makes these devices good for dense soils, but not light, sandy soils.

■ **Long, Strong Screwdriver:** A long screwdriver can be pushed to depths over one foot. They are great for an overall impression, but lack the specifics because it is difficult to tell the depth of the soil it brings up.

■ **Tensiometers:** These devices measure how strongly water is held in soil. They are most commonly used in agriculture and in landscapes where evenly moist soils are desired; they tend to fail in dry, coarse soils.

All these instruments can be used to gauge soil moisture: a long screwdriver, wooden dowel, knife, hand trowel, moisture meter, and a thin-walled pipe, hammer and rebar.

How To Identify a Water Problem

Whether home enthusiast or professional landscaper, every gardener needs to know the signs of water problems. Below are the most common characteristics of too much water and too little.

Too Wet: Compacted, Overwatered, Low Oxygen Environments

Saturated soils breed a slew of problems. They cause oxygen levels to fall, acidity to increase, and plant health to plummet. As plant health falls, so does its resistance to funguses, insects and weeds. In addition, too much summer irrigation shortens the life of many California Friendly plants. Many of these plants evolved to summer dormancy and overwatering encourages them to keep growing rather than rest.

Signs

- Wilting and drooping flowers, leaves and stems.
- Limp (not brittle) leaves.
- Edema (a blister-like symptom on the fleshy parts).
- Translucent or grey-hued leaves.
- Irregular and rangy growth.
- Limp, stunted growth.
- Persistent infestations of fungus.
- Lots of vegetative growth, but little flower or fruit.
- A sour (not sweet) smell to the soil.
- Algae, mold or moss.

Remedies

- Shut off irrigation.
- Plant water loving plants in perpetually moist areas.
- Mix organic matter into soil.
- Direct sheeting or running water away from area.

Swollen leaves and lanky growth indicates this *Euphorbia tirucalli* is getting too much water.

Weeds that Indicate Too Much Moisture

Chickweed, clover, dandelion, dichondra, dock, English daisy, nutgrass, oxalis, pennywort and plantain.

Nutgrass (*Cyperus* spp.) is not compatible to the conditions that favor rosemary and yucca. Its presence indicates this landscape is being over-irrigated.

Too Dry

Every plant needs water at some point, and without it the plant will show visible signs of distress. A lack of water not only shuts down a plant's essential functions, like photosynthesis, gas exchange and rigidity, but also shuts down the biological activity in the soil, decreasing levels of nutrients, increasing levels of salts, and reducing the soils ability to physically hold the moisture it does get.

Signs

- Wilting and drooping flowers, leafs and stems.
- Brittle (not limp) leaves.
- Dull, bluish leaves.
- Shedding of older leaves.
- Burns around the leaf edges.
- Extensive leaf drop.
- Stunted new growth.

This patch of *Aloe striata* is showing the signs of under-watering with shriveled leaves, dying older leaves, and stunted new growth.

Remedies

- Recharge the soil with irrigation.
- Recalibrate irrigation schedule to avoid stressing the landscape.
- Apply humus to reduce salt's affects and wood chips to reduce soil temperatures and evaporation.
- If heavy with salts, leach soil with deep, deep watering.

Weeds that Indicate Dry Conditions

Cheeseweed (mallow), crabgrass, horseweed, lamb's quarters, prickly lettuce, purslane, spotted spurge, sweet fennel, thistles and tumbleweed.

Soil can be read by its weeds. The horehound and tumbleweed pictured above not only indicate dry soil but also the presence of organic matter and salt.

Repellency Layer

Organic oils, resins, and waxes—residues from plants—accumulate in soils. These hydrocarbons begin evaporating as the soil becomes parched. Some of these gases will eventually condense, coating soil particles with a waxy layer, creating an impermeable barrier. When irrigation hits soils with this hydrophobic layer it beads up and runs off, never infiltrating. Repellency layers not only make irrigation difficult, but will also increase chances of runoff and topsoil loss.

A hydrophobic layer is common after wildfires and in times of intense heat. Sandy soils are more prone to repellency than clay because sand has less surface area than clay.

The remedies for breaking repellency include turning over the top 2" of soil with a shovel, scratching the soil with a stiff rake, mixing clay into the soil, applying pulse irrigation (brief irrigation many times a day), and mulching the soil to cool it and provide a water holding layer.

The small puddle of water pictured has been sitting on this sandy soil for over five minutes. A repellency layer has stopped it from infiltrating. Water repellence is more common in sandy soils that grow resinous plants.

Controlling
Your Controller

Irrigation controllers and timers maintain the functional
success of plants and landscapes without the hassle of
hand watering or manually turning on the system. They are
undoubtedly convenient, but, unfortunately, most automatic
controllers tend to overwater. They do not irrigate to current
conditions and water needs because they have not been
programmed correctly and attentively.

Programming a controller/timer requires time and some math. There's no way around it. If programmed properly, irrigation will go on when a soil dries to a predetermined depth and then replenish the moisture lost. For example, if a bed of shrubs and perennials dries to 6", then the irrigation will water to 6" deep. The interval between watering should be the length of time it takes the soil to dry to 6" again.

Quick Tips for Controlling the Controller

Programming a controller is not a process you want to rush. Taking the time to do it right will save time in the long run. Following are some tips to help you off to a good start:

- Raise the controller off the ground and either install it at seating level (about 3.5') or standing level (about 5').

- Put the controller where there are views of the landscape.

- Put the controller in the shade.

- Put valve names and run times in both English and Spanish.

- For rapid control, put an on/off switch between the controller and each valve.

- And finally—expect and budget the time necessary to update the controller once a month.

The position of this controller indicates a weak commitment to water conservation. It is tucked into the far corner of the property, irrigators need to be on their knees with their backs turned to the landscape to use it, and there is no shade.

This chapter covers the steps necessary to ensure that the controller accurately reflects current conditions and needs. There are two basic questions to answer when programming a controller. The first is how much to water. The second is how often to water. This chapter is devoted to answering those two questions.

1. How Much to Water?

To determine how much irrigation is needed you need to figure out the length of time a valve should be turned on. Valve run time is a product of watering goal, type of soil, and type of delivery device. The watering goal is the depth of soil that you want the irrigation to penetrate. The type of soil influences the amount of water required. Finally, the type of watering device used determines the rate at which water is delivered. This can be reduced to a simple formula:

Run Time = Water Goal / Rate of Delivery

Watering Goal

The watering goal is the depth to which you want water to penetrate. This goal will change with time. It will vary depending on the season of the year and the maturity of the landscape.

If an irrigation valve is irrigating a single type of plant, then determining the water goal is easy: look up its "dry-to depth" in a Plant chapter. Dry-To depths are the watering goal.

If many plants are on one irrigation valve, then one of those plants must be selected as the base plant to obtain a dry-to depth. As illustrated in the scenarios below, there is no one right way to select the base plant. Here are a few methods:

- Pick the plant used in the greatest number within the area covered by the valve.
- Pick the plant with the lowest water requirements.
- Pick the plant that provides the greatest benefit/function, such as shade or screening.
- Get a base average from all the plants' dry-to depths.

This area is irrigated with one valve and includes *Senecio*, agave, fountain grass and 3 trees, a locust, eucalyptus and live oak. What plant would you irrigate to? The grass is the most water needy, the oak and Eucalyptus the least. Watering to the grass overwaters all else; irrigating to the trees will cause all others to suffer. The Grand Park, Los Angeles.

Type of Soil

The type of soil greatly affects the amount of water required and the rate at which the soil can receive it. Clay soils may need as much as twice the water and time as sandy soils. The watering times below are based on dry soils. Moist or wet soils should be dried before using these recommendations. Another thing to keep in mind is that soils that are reluctant to receive water, such as clay, are also reluctant to lose it. Even in the middle of summer it can take clay soils weeks to dry.

Quick Note: *1 inch of water over 1 sq. ft. equals 0.623 gallons of water* ■

Chart 1: Amount of Water Required and Rates of Maximum Delivery per any sq. ft.*

Watering Depth / Dry-To Depth	Course (sandy loam) Amount of Water Amount of Time	Medium (silt) Amount of Water Amount of Time	Fine (clay loam) Amount of Water Amount of Time
3"	Needs: .25" Takes: 1–2 minutes	Needs: .375" Takes: 4–5 minutes	Needs: .5" Takes: 8 minutes
4"	Needs: .33" Takes: 2–3 minutes	Needs: .48" Takes: 7–8 minutes	Needs: .66" Takes: 20 minutes
5"	Needs: .42" Takes: 3–4 minutes	Needs: .59" Takes: 10 minutes	Needs: .83" Takes: 36 minutes
6"	Needs: .5" Takes: 4–5 minutes	Needs: .75" Takes: 13 minutes	Needs: 1" Takes: 60 minutes
9"	Needs: .75" Takes: 12 minutes	Needs: 1.25" Takes: 25 minutes	Needs: 1.5" Takes: 1 hour and 30 minutes
1'	Needs: 1" Takes: 18 minutes	Needs: 1.5" Takes: 36 minutes	Needs: 2.1" Takes: 2 hours and 15 minutes
1.5'	Needs: 1.5" Takes: 26 minutes	Needs: 2.25" Takes: 48 minutes	Needs: 3" Takes: 3 hours
2.25'	Needs: 2.25" Takes: 42 minutes	Needs: 3.37" Takes: 1 hour and 15 minutes	Needs: 4.5" Takes: 4 hours and 50 minutes
3'	Needs: 3" Takes: 1 hour and 6 minutes	Needs: 4.5" Takes: 1 hour and 45 minutes	Needs: 6.5" Takes: 7 hours and 10 minutes

*Bear in mind that your municipality may have watering restrictions during drought or critical shortages and that you will need to water in intervals within local watering restrictions.

Chart 2: Gallons of Water Needed in Dry Soil per 200 sq. ft.

Watering Depth	Course: Sandy Loam	Medium: Silt	Fine: Clay
3"	31	47	63
4"	41	60	83
5"	53	74	104
6"	63	94	125
9"	94	157	188
1'	125	188	263
1.5'	188	282	376
2.25'	282	423	564
3'	376	564	815

Watering Device

The next step in determining valve run times is finding out how much water your existing system delivers. High-pressure sprinklers deliver water between 0.5 to 20 gallons per minute (gpm). Low-pressure devices, like inline emitters and micro-spray heads, deliver water between 0.5 to 4 gallons per hour (gph).

To figure how many gallons a device delivers per sq. ft. divide its gpm or gph by the area it covers in sq. ft. If gph, then divide the total by 60 to get gallons per minute.

High Pressure: ___ gpm / ___ sq. ft. covered = _____ gallons per sq. ft. per minute

Low Pressure: ___ gph / ___ sq. ft. covered / 60 = ___ gallons per sq. ft. per minute

Example 1: A sprinkler head that delivers water at 2 gpm and covers 70 sq. ft. delivers 0.03 gallons per sq. ft. per minute.

Example 2: The emitters in the tubing deliver water at 0.5 gph and cover 0.75 sq. ft., delivers 0.01 gallons per sq. ft. per minute.

Inline emitter tubing being installed a couple inches below ground. Courtesy of Camrosa Water District.

There are three ways to determine the amount of water a device delivers. The list is ranked from most to least accurate.

1. Take measurements. If the system uses overhead sprinklers, place cups within its radius, run irrigation for 10 minutes and measure collected amounts; if it uses low-pressure, place cups under the devices, run for 20 minutes and measure collected amounts.

2. Read the stamp on the device. Many devices have imprints or prints signifying the rates of delivery, but be aware that age and use change those rates dramatically.

3. Identify the product and search the Internet for specifications. Be aware, though, that these specifications are usually expressed as a range, and it is difficult to pinpoint a specific performance.

Emitter Wetting Patterns

The emitter wetting patterns vary and are a product of the type of soil and the watering depth. The greater the depth, the greater the horizontal spread of water. The absolute best way to find out the wetting pattern is to physically examine the soil: turn on the irrigation for 20 minutes, turn off and wait for two hours, and then dig to the edges and bottom of the wetting pattern to determine its size.

Another method of determining the wetting pattern of emitters is a rough calculation. In sandy soil emitters spread 1 times the depth; irrigating 6" down wets 6 sq. inches. In silt soils the wetting patterns is 2 times depth; 6" down wets 1 sq. ft. In clay soil water spreads 4 times the depth; 6" down wets 2 sq. ft.

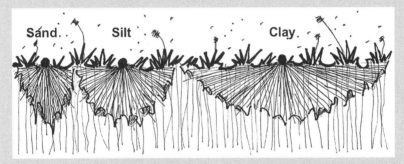

Type of soil greatly impacts the amount of water needed and its horizontal spread. Irrigating 1 square foot to 4" deep requires 0.205 gallons of water in sandy soils, 0.300 in silty soils, and 0.415 in clay soils.

As an Example

Let's say you have two valves to irrigate an area with a mass of ground covers. One valve is low-pressure inline emitter tubing and the other is rotor sprinkler heads. The soil was determined to be silt and the ideal watering depth for the ground cover is 5".

As a reminder: *1" of water per sq. ft. equals 0.623 gallons of water.* ∎

Valve 1: This valve is comprised of inline emitter tubing that delivers water at 1 gph. According to the information above this emitter wets 1 sq. ft. Using Chart 1 we see that watering to 5" in silt requires 0.59 inches of water per sq. ft.

The Numbers

Need 0.59 inches = 0.59" * .623 = .37 gallons per sq. ft.

Device delivers 1 gph over 1 sq. ft. (1/60) = .0167 gallons per minute

= .37 gallons (needed) /0 .0167 (delivered) = 22 minutes

Valve 2: This valve has rotor heads that delivers water at 2 gpm. One head covers 60 sq. ft. According to Chart 1 watering to 5" in silt requires 0.59 inches of water per sq. ft.

The Numbers

Need .59 inches = .59" * .623 = .37 gallons per sq ft.

Device Delivers 2 gpm over 60 sq. ft. (2/60) = .033 gallons per minute

= .37 gallons (needed) / 0.033 (delivered) = 11 minutes

Pulse Irrigation

Delivery devices may supply water faster than a soil can absorb it. If that is the case pulse irrigation is the remedy. Pulse irrigation works by irrigating the top 2" of soil, where infiltration occurs quickly, stopping irrigation for several hours, and then watering the top 2" again. Getting water to 6" deep with this practice might require 3 pulses, that is, 3 cycles of brief irrigation. Pulse irrigation is often used on slopes and areas with dense soils.

This slope needs pulse irrigation. Rills at the top of the photo and a buried mow strip at the bottom mean that the slope is getting water faster than it can accept it.

2. How Often to Water?

To figure out how often to water you need to know how long it takes a particular soil to dry out. There are many books, formulas, and online calculators that help determine the interval between irrigation, but none are as accurate as physical measurements.

The best way to determine drying times is to wet the landscape, turn off the irrigation, and take soil samples every two to four days. Continue taking soil samples until the soil dries to the base plant's dry-to depth, at which point you have the number days between watering. Although these tests should be performed every several months, they are especially important in spring and late summer, when irrigation plays a pivotal role in both plant health and regional conservation.

Despite the soil looking dry both the moisture meter and wooden dowel indicate that there is plenty of moisture 4" down.

Best Time of Day to Irrigate

Landscapes along the coast should be irrigated early morning to reduce chances of mildew and rot. Landscapes in the drier foothills, mountains and deserts should be irrigated mid-evening to minimize water loss to evaporation. Also, try to have the irrigation go on when someone is around to observe. Broken irrigation or overspray will persist for weeks if no one notices.

Weather-Based Timers

A weather-based timer calculates your landscape's water needs according to the weather and then turns on the valves individually to meet the demands of each hydrozone. The timer does this by taking the information you give it about your landscape and combining that with information it gets from the nearest weather station.

Weather-based timers are the most efficient irrigation controller for established landscapes, large lots, and gardens close to a weather station. The timer is a little unyielding for gardens that change a lot, and for those where the weather station is in a different microclimate. In order for the timer to work properly—that is, maintain plant health without wasting water—it needs accurate and timely information. This means someone must change the timer's information every time a change occurs in the landscape.

Budget Adjustment

A feature rarely used on irrigation controllers (despite the fact that most have them) is the budget adjuster. This feature allows you to turn the entire irrigation system up or down by percentages, instead of reprogramming each station. These adjustments are handy when unusual weather happens, such as summer fog or rain.

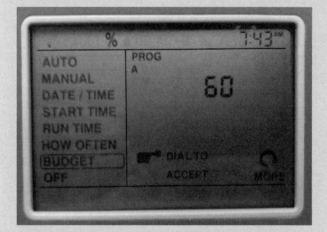

The budget adjustment feature on your automatic irrigation controller is a quick way to respond to changing conditions. Mid-summer monsoon? Reduce all irrigation by 60%. June gloom in July? Reduce all irrigation by 40%. Budget adjustment allows for quick control of all irrigation valves.

Troubleshooting Irrigation Controllers

Controller Will Not Keep a Program

Why: A controller reverts back to pre-programmed settings.

Remedy: Replace the controller's battery and either replace the timer's plug or the structure's outlet.

The Irrigation System is Always Over or Underwatering

Why: The gardener is not giving the controller accurate information.

Remedy: Install a weather-based controller, or install a rain gauge and/or moisture sensors. Always, remember to water with any local watering restrictions.

The Irrigation System Comes on in the Rain

Remedy: Install an inexpensive rain sensor.

The Irrigation System Runs Despite Breaks in the Line

Remedy: Install a flow sensor before the manifolds. These sensors detect irregularities and will shut off the problem valve.

Too Many Stations to Re-Program Individually During Shift in Weather

Remedy: Use the Water Budget feature. This feature will cut watering to all stations by a certain percentage. Overcast? Reduce irrigation by 20%. A light summer rain? Reduce irrigation by 80%.

or

Alternative Remedy: Install on/off switches between the controller and each valve.

Pulling It All Together: 3 Examples

California Lilac (*Ceanothus gloriosus*) in sand

	Spring	Summer	Fall	Winter
Watering Depth	6"	6"	1'	0
Soil	Sand			
Water Needed: gallons per sq. ft.	0.5" = 0.31 gallons (.5*.623)	0.5" = 0.31 gallons (.5*.623)	1" = 0.623 gallons (1*.623)	0
Time to Infiltrate	5 minutes	5 minutes	18 minutes	0
Rate of Delivery	Emitter: 2 gph	Emitter: 2 gph	Emitter: 2 gph	Emitter: 2 gph
Wetting Pattern	6 sq. inches	6 sq. inches	1 sq. ft.	0
Delivery per sq. ft. per minute	0.067 gallons (2/60/.5)	0.067 gallons (2/60/.5)	0.033 gallons (2/60/1)	0
Time Needed	4.6 minutes (.31 / .067)	4.6 minutes (.31 / .063)	9 minutes (.623 / .033)	
Pulses	0	0	0	0
Valve Run Time	5 minutes	5 minutes	19 minutes	0
Dry Time*	6 days	4 days	6 days	0

* Dry Time is a product of observation and soil tests.

Coral Bells (*Heuchera spp.*) in clay

	Spring	Summer	Fall	Winter
Watering Depth	4"	6"	6'	0
Soil	Clay			
Water Needed: gallons per sq. ft.	0.66" = 0.41 gallons (.66*.623)	1" = 0.623 gallons (1*.623)	1" = 0.623 gallons (1*.623)	0
Time to Infiltrate	20 minutes	60 minutes	60 minutes	0
Rate of Delivery	Rotor Head: 2 gpm	Rotor Head: 2 gpm	Rotor Head: 2 gpm	Rotor Head: 2 gpm
Wetting Pattern	60 sq. ft.	60 sq. ft.	60 sq. ft.	0
Delivery per sq. ft. per minute	0.033 gallons (2/60)	0.033 gallons (2/60)	0.033 gallons (2/60)	0
Time Needed	12 minutes (.41 / .033)	19 minutes (.623 / .033)	19 minutes (.623 / .033)	
Pulses**	2	4	4	0
Valve Run Time	6 minutes / 2 times	5 minutes / 4 times	5 minutes / 4 times	0
Watering Interval/ Dry Time*	6 days	8 days	11 days	0

* Dry Time is a product of observation and soil tests.

** Pulses are needed because Time to Infiltrate exceeds Time Needed, meaning these heads deliver water faster than the soil can absorb it.

California Fescue (*Festuca californica*) in clay

	Spring	Summer	Fall	Winter
Watering Depth	4"	6"	6"	4"
Soil	Clay			
Water Needed: gallons per sq. ft.	0.66" = 0.41 gallons per sq. ft. (.66*.623)	1" = 0.623 gallons per sq. ft. (1*.623)	1" = 0.623 gallons per sq. ft. (1*.623)	0.66" = 0.41 gallons per sq. ft. (.66*.623)
Time to Infiltrate	20 minutes	60 minutes	60 minutes	20 minutes
Rate of Delivery	Emitter: .5 gph	Emitter: .5 gph	Emitter: .5 gph	Emitter: .5 gph
Wetting Pattern	1.5 sq. ft.	2 sq. ft.	2 sq. ft.	1.5 sq. ft.
Delivery per sq. ft. per minute	0.005 gallons (.5/60/1.5)	0.004 gallons (.5/60/2)	0.004 gallons (.5/60/2)	0.005 gallons (.5/60/1.5)
Time Needed	82 minutes (.41 / .005)	157 minutes (.623 / .004)	157 minutes (.623 / .004)	82 minutes (.41 / .005)
Pulses	0	0	0	0
Valve Run Time	82 minutes	157 minutes	157 minutes	82
Dry Time*	6 days	9 days	11 days	20 days

* Dry Time is a product of observation and soil tests.

4

Irrigation Maintenance and Troubleshooting

The key to effective water management is budgeting the time and resources needed to run an efficient irrigation system. This chapter is designed to help you make the most of maintenance time. It covers the most common problems with high and low-pressure irrigation systems and provides a seasonal calendar for routine tasks.

Biggest Time Savers

Uniformity: When you need to replace a water delivery device, always use one that matches the performance of the other devices on the line. Using devices with dissimilar rates of delivery will create wet/dry spots, reduce plant health, and increase frustration because the landscape is not performing as planned.

Cleanliness: Always flush a line after a repair is made. A clogged head will not only change the performance of that particular device, but will affect the entire line as well.

Pressure: Water pressure affects irrigation performance. Water pressure is managed at the manifold and along the entire line. Use too much pressure and sprinkler heads will mist (wasting a lot of water) and delivery devices and connectors will pop apart. Use too little pressure and water will be distributed unevenly which slows or stops mechanical devices, such as manifolds, impact heads, and rotor devices.

Control the Controller: An irrigation controller is only as good as the information it receives. A controller should be updated with new information at least four times a year; once a month would be preferable.

Flush and Filter: Low-pressure irrigation systems are especially prone to clogging. Filters should be checked and cleaned monthly and the system flushed no less than twice a year, preferably in late winter and

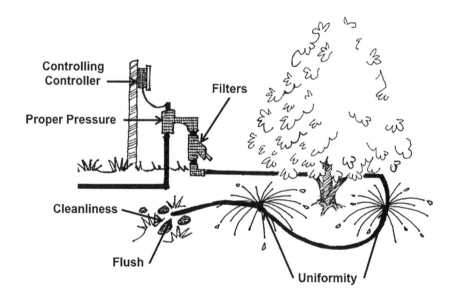

late summer. If the irrigation water has minerals and salts (leaving a white film or plating), then it may require an acid flushing. The most common acid flush is muriatic acid. Clogged heads can be soaked in vinegar to remove deposits. Maintaining the filters and flushing the system will increase the longevity of the system and save time in the long run.

Common Problems and Troubleshooting

This section lists the primary problems with high-pressure systems, low-pressure systems and the irrigation manifolds. The previous chapter, *Controlling Your Controller*, described common problems with controllers.

Awake and Aware

A busted sprinkler on a residential lot can gush between 3 and 5 gallons of water a minute; the larger diameter pipes on commercial properties can easily triple that. For instance, a busted head on a typical residential property that ran for 10 minutes twice a week would waste as much as 80 gallons a week; the loss on a commercial lot could be as much as 300 gallons a week.

One of the easiest strategies for minimizing the impact of broken heads is to have the irrigation go on when someone is around, awake and available to take prompt action. If this is not possible, the system must be run and examined at least once a month. Properly budgeting the time and expense of diagnostics is essential to water management.

High Pressure Problems

High-pressure irrigation systems are designed to distribute water over a large area in a short period of time. These systems use rotor heads, impact spray heads, regular spray heads and bubblers. The common problems that plague these types of systems are listed below, as is their best remedies.

Broken Heads, Leaky Seals and Fittings

Cause: Equipment ages, wears, or is poorly maintained.

Remedy: Replace faulty parts.

Erratic and Irregular Spray Patterns

Cause: Spray heads become clogged with particles and mineral deposits. This often occurs after work has been done on the line.

Remedy: Clean or replace filters and clean sprinkler head with a soft bristle brush or pipe cleaner (never with metal scarring devices, such as screwdrivers or wires), or replace head. If there is a lot of debris in the line, remove the last sprinkler, reduce line pressure at the valve and flush the debris by running the irrigation for several minutes.

Irregular Distribution of Water

Areas that are either too wet or too dry along a single line can occur for a number of reasons. The three listed below are the most common.

Cause: A sprinkler head was not replaced with one that matches the performance of the existing heads.

Remedy: Make sure that all new heads match the performance of the existing system.

Cause: The distance between the sprinkler heads is irregular, causing dryness in some areas and pooling in others.

Remedy: Dig up irrigation and re-install sprinkler heads, ensuring that both rate and distance are constant.

Cause: The environment has changed along one line due to factors such as change in amount of sun the area receives or the addition or substitution of different plants with different watering needs.

Remedies: Identify hydrozones and run new lines to them, or change individual heads to meet the performance needs of the immediate area (such as low-pressure in the shade and high-pressure in the sun), or try altering the environment (such as removing or pruning plants to reduce water needs).

Irregular Distribution of Water on Slopes

Cause: The pressure is always greater downhill.

Remedy: Replace lower heads with pressure regulating heads.

Misting

Cause: Heads are turned down too low or there is too much pressure (up to 50% of the irrigation can be lost to evaporation and wind drift in misting conditions).

Remedies: Install a pressure regulator just past the manifold, or replace sprinkler head with one rated for the psi.

The street and driveway are noticeably wet. The mist produced from these sprinkler heads has been caught by the wind. The water pressure needs to be reduced and/or the heads replaced.

Pooling Water Due to Slow Rotor Heads or Impact Sprinklers

Cause: Mechanically driven devices need a minimum amount of water pressure to operate properly; low pressure can stall a device.

Remedies: Check to make sure the pressure is up at the valve, replace head with one requiring less pressure, or remove one or two heads from the line to increase overall pressure.

Pooling Water Around Low Heads

Cause: Water always pools around the lowest lying sprinkler as the system drains to that point.

Remedies: Raise the heads, install heads with check-valves, or create a lower point in the line.

The sprinkler head pictured continues to dribble water long after the valve has been shut off. The ruts in the soil as a result are obvious. The remedies are to install a sprinkler head with a check valve, raise the head, or shore up the slope around the head with large drain rock.

Run Off

Cause: Sprinkler-caused runoff occurs either because the spray pattern is watering impermeable surfaces or the soil has reached its saturation point.

Remedies: Test spray pattern and fix overspray, or use pulse irrigation to irrigate areas prone to pooling and runoff. See the previous chapter *Controlling Your Controller* for a description of Pulse Irrigation.

Spray Deflection

Cause: Vegetation grows around sprinklers and obstructs and deflects spray.

Remedies: Prune vegetation, substitute lower-growing plants, change to drip irrigation, or change location of sprinkler.

Spray Distance is Weak

Cause: Weak flow occurs because of an undetected leak, a clogged manifold, or a drop in the water pressure.

Remedies: Look for a leak, ensure flow at the manifold, and clean the sprinklers, or remove some sprinklers from the line to increase line pressure.

Sunken Sprinklers

Cause: Healthy landscapes produce topsoil and over time it builds up and around a sprinkler, causing obstruction and deflection.

Remedies: Raise sprinklers, or lower grade of landscape.

Low Pressure Problems

Designed to reduce inefficiencies and water loss, low-pressure irrigation delivers water directly to where the plant needs it. These systems use drip (micro-sprayers, bubblers, emitters), inline emitter tubing, and soaker hose. The common problems that plague these types of systems are listed below, as is their best remedies.

Connectors, Fittings and/or Delivery Devices Pop Off

Cause: The pressure is too high in the system.

Remedy: Install a pressure regulator just before the manifold.

Cracking in Hose or Soaker Tube

Cause: Age, wear, exposure to sun, and temperature changes can all cause a hose to crack and open under pressure.

Remedies: Replace fractured, brittle sections of the hose and mulch regularly or bury hose.

Drippers, Emitters or Misters are Clogged

Cause: Systems without filters and/or self-cleaning heads are naturally prone to clogging.

Remedies: Clean filter or install filter just below the manifold, remove end-caps and flush the system, and clear obstruction or replace device.

Note: *Switching water supply, such as to reclaimed or well water, will increase particles in water and without a filter the system will become more prone to blockage.* ▨

Dry Soil and Signs of Plant Stress Along Entire Line

Cause: The line may not be running long enough, the heads may be clogged, or there could be an undetected break in the line.

Remedies: Look for a leak, and double check the valve's run time and interval between watering. Then run the system and check performance of heads.

Leaks that are Reoccurring in Lateral Lines

Cause: Animals bite into tubing seeking water and damage it. This problem is especially common in summer and fall.

Remedies: Repair leaks, bury hose under 2" of soil and 3" to 4" of woody mulch.

Uneven Distribution of Water

Cause: Emitter hose, micro-sprays and soaker tubing will produce an uneven flow of water if the line's pressure is too low, the ground is too uneven, or the hose takes too many bends and curves.

Remedies: To increase the pressure in the line check the flow control screw, straighten the path of the hose, run the hose across a slope instead of down it, or remove some of the water devices to increase pressure.

Weeds Right Along the Hose

Cause: In dry landscapes weeds grow where the water is, which is typically right along the hose.

Remedies: Maintain a 2" to 4" layer of wood chips or woody mulch. Also avoid walking in the area because it compacts the mulch and sets the seeds.

Manifold / Valve Problems

The manifold is a device that controls the flow of water from its source to the irrigation line. Manifolds can fail and their most commons problems, along with the best remedies, are listed below.

Automatic Manifold Will Not Shut Off

Cause: There are a slew of reasons why a manifold may not shut off and three of them are below.

1. The flow control screw may be tightened too far, which is common when a conventional system has been converted to low-flow. Manifolds need a certain level of pressure to operate properly.
Remedy: Install a pressure regulator immediately after the manifold and turn the valve's pressure back up.
2. The controller is producing a constant charge. This is identifiable by a warm solenoid.
Remedy: Fix or replace the irrigation controller.
3. The solenoid is damaged. This is identifiable by a small but constant flow of water through the manifold.
Remedy: Replace the solenoid plunger and its seat.

Automatic Manifold Will Not Turn On

Cause: There are two reasons why a manifold may not turn on.

1. The flow control screw may be tightened all way.
Remedy: Loosen flow control screw.
2. The solenoid is not receiving a charge.
Cause: There is a cut in the irrigation wire, the wires have rusted in the wirenuts, the solenoid is broken, or the controller is not sending a signal (the least likely cause).
Remedy: Run an electrical diagnostic and repair damage.

Seasonal Maintenance Calendar

Every type of irrigation system benefits from routine, preventive maintenance. The seasonal tasks listed below will not only improve the efficiency of your irrigation system, but extend its life too.

Spring

- Turn On / Adjust controllers.
- Replace batteries in controllers.

High Pressure Systems

- Adjust spray patterns and unclog heads.

Low Pressure Systems

- Unscrew end-caps and flush debris.

Note: It is important to avoid working on wet soil. Soils compaction leads to all types of problems: low oxygen, changing levels of pH, noxious weeds, and poor plant health. ■

Summer

- Adjust controllers to warming conditions.
- Modify, upgrade or fix the system after soil has dried.

High Pressure Systems

- Prune or replace plants that block spray.
- Repair or replace broken heads.

Low Pressure Systems

- Mulch for sun protection.

Note: Southern California gets summer rains and periods of intense humidity; it is important to turn off automatic controllers during these times to avoid fungus and rot. ■

Fall

■ Adjust controllers: many Mediterranean plants go dormant this time of year and syncing irrigation to plant needs is essential.

High Pressure Systems

■ Repair or replace broken heads.

■ Adjust spray patterns and unclog heads.

■ Run and check all axillary motors, valves and emergency devices.

Low Pressure Systems

■ Bury and protect lines from rodents.

■ Unscrew end-caps and flush of debris.

Winter

■ Turn off or adjust controllers for minimal water needs.

Both Systems

■ Winterize: In areas of freeze drain pipes and hoses of water, and insulate manifolds and any above-ground mainlines.

Low Pressure Systems

■ If irrigating with hard water, flush system with an acid based solution. The acid will help dissolve deposits and improve systems performance and longevity.

■ Remove clogged spray heads and emitters and soak them in vinegar to clean.

5

Irrigating With Recycled Water

Recycled wastewater is one of the fastest growing sources of new water in Southern California. Recycled water irrigates commercial complexes, college campuses and residential communities—tens of thousands of acres in all. Recycled water is also referred to as reclaimed water, treated wastewater, or purple-pipe water.

Recycled water is different than other types of water used in a landscape. It is more alkaline and has more salt. Recycled water that irrigates urban landscapes has probably gone through tertiary treatment, which is fairly extensive. Primary treatment removes the large solids, secondary treatment uses microorganisms to remove most of the remaining solids, and tertiary treatment involves filtration and disinfection (usually chlorine). Recycled water does not pose a health risk to humans or pets.

Chemical Composition of Urban Waters

	Ammonia Nitrogen	Nitrite Nitrogen	Alkalinity	Chloride	Hardness	pH
Tap Water	0.4	0.15	180	120	240	7
Recycled Water	0.2	0.15	340	120	180	7.5
Roof Rainwater	3.5	0.15	15	15	28	6.7
Field Rainwater	3.5	0.15	30	15	30	6.5

James Crook, Ph.D., P.E. *Technical Memorandum on Graywater.* On behalf of Clean Water Coalition and Southern Nevada Water Authority. February 2009.

Recycled water is chemically different, and therefore it needs to be used differently. For the best results, follow the recommendations below.

1. Deep and Infrequent Irrigation: Allows soils to dry to their dry-to depth (see the Irrigation chapters) and then deeply water to move salts. This method of irrigation also allows soils to open up, breathe, and exchange its gases.

2. Leach: Because frequent watering schedules and low-flow devices struggle to move salts through the soil, leaching is sometimes necessary. Leaching is the process of drenching the soil, allowing it to dry out, and then drenching it again. Typically, rainwater leaches the soil, but in times of drought, flushing with piped water may be necessary. Late winter through early spring is the best times to leach the soil.

3. Use Less Fertilizer: Many of the richest fertilizers—the chemicals and derivatives of animal products—contain salts. Using these types of fertilizers can compound existing salt problems. If nutrient deficiencies are evident, fertilize with compost, humus or other aged organics.

4. Screening: If pumping recycled water through low-flow devices, such as emitter tubing, use fine filters to screen the water. It will improve system longevity. These screens will need to be cleaned at least annually, and more frequently if the water is particularly hard

5. Use Salt-Tolerant Plants: Despite taking corrective measures, some plants will not respond well to recycled water. Many, however, will thrive. See the Plant section at the end of this chapter for more information.

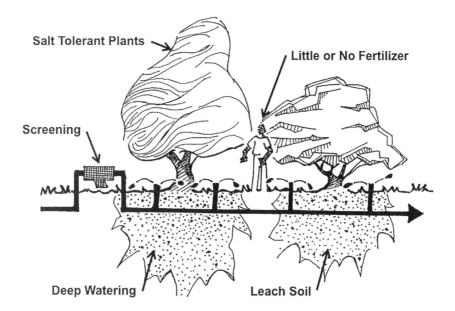

Plants

Studies on the effects of recycled water on plants have found that most plants are not greatly affected, especially if the recycled water is supplemented with fresh. When recycled water affects a plant, it is usually the salts that cause the problems. As a rule acid-loving plants struggle; deciduous plants do better than evergreen (though many tropical plants are an exception); and plants that occur naturally along dry streams that seasonally flood may thrive.

Continued on page 50

Desiccation and Alkalinity

Using recycled water improperly causes salts to accumulate in the soil, and the pH to climb. This creates alkaline soil that can desiccate plants. When evaporation exceeds irrigation, salts will not be leach beyond plant roots, and the soil starts sucking water from plants, slowly killing them. Alkaline soils create another problem. They tie up iron, making it unavailable to plants, creating chlorosis, which slowly kills plants.

Both the accumulation of salts and alkalinity have visible signs. They will be most evident with plants poorly adapted to those conditions. Below are the signs of too much salt and alkalinity.

Signs

- Burns around the leaf edge.
- Shedding of older leaves.
- Wilting and drooping flowers, leaves and stems.
- Brittle, crunchy, rigid leaves.
- Dull, bluish leaves without sheen.
- Chlorosis (yellow leaves with green veins) caused by a lack of chlorophyll.
- Cracked and split bark.
- Stunted new growth.

The leaves pictured are showing the signs of desiccation: scorched leaves.

General Remedies

- Leach soil with deep, deep watering.

- Apply humus and/or finely composted mulch regularly.

- Reduce or stop the use of fertilizers.

- And, if salts are severe, then along with the humus, work gypsum or sulfur into soil.

Remedies Specifically for Iron Chlorosis

Neutral or alkaline soils tend to lock up iron, making it unavailable to plants. To fix the problem:

- Add a lot of rich humus, which will help acidify the soil.

- Work iron additives into the soil—up to 2 pounds per acre.

- If the problem is widespread, treat with a foliar application of iron.

This young California black walnut is showing the signs of iron deficiency and chlorosis: yellow leaves with green veins.

In this beautiful and simple setting, the blue agave, red yucca and trailing rosemary are thriving with recycled water. Orange County Coastkeeper's Natural Play Garden, Orange.

The lists of plants below have shown tolerance to salts and alkalinity.

Plants with tolerance to salts and alkalinity

Trees
Acacia spp. Acacia
Aesculus californica California buckeye
Arbutus unedo Strawberry tree
Fraxinus spp. Ash
Betula spp. Birch
Cassia spp. Golden shower, Gold medallion
Ceratonia siliqua Carob
Cinnamomum camphora Camphor
Eucalyptus spp. Eucalyptus
Ficus spp. Ficus
Gingko biloba Maidenhair tree
Liquidambar spp. Sweet gum
Melaleuca spp. Melaleuca
Palms Palms
Pistacia chinensis Chinese pistache
Prosopis spp. Mesquite
Prunus spp. Cherries and Laurel
Quercus spp. Oak: deciduous and shrub varieties
Robinia pseudoacacia Black locust
Salix spp. Willow
Sambucus spp. Elderberry

Ulmus parvifolia Chinese elm
Umbellularia californica California bay

Shrubs

Arctostaphylos spp. Manzanita
Artemisia spp. Artemisia
Baccharis pilularis Coyote brush
Carrisa spp. Natal plum
Ceanothus spp. California lilac
Cistus spp. Rockrose
Cotoneaster spp. Cotoneaster
Ilex spp. Holly
Juniperus spp. Juniper
Lantana spp. Lantana
Myoporum spp. Myoporum
Nerium oleander Oleander
Pittosporum spp. Pittosporum
Rhaphiolepis spp. Indian hawthorne
Rhus integrifolia Lemonade berry
Rosmarinus officinalis Rosemary

Perennials

Achillea spp. Yarrow
Agapanthus spp. Lily-of-the-Nile
Arctotheca calendula Capeweed
Armeria maritime Thrift
Bamboo Bamboo
Convolvulus mauritanicus, C. sabatius Ground morning glory
Echinacea purpurea Purple coneflower
Echium spp. Pride of Madeira, Tower of jewels
Erigeron glaucus Seaside daisy
Euryops spp. Euryops
Gazania hybrids Gazania
Grindelia hirsutula Gumplant
Hypericum spp. St. John's wort
Lavandula spp. Lavender
Lessingia filaginifolia 'Silver Carpet' California beach aster
Limonium perezii Sea lavender
Penstemon spp. Bearded tongue
Santolina chamaecyparissus Lavender cotton
Stachys byzantina Lamb's ears
Tropaeolum spp. Nasturtium

Vines

Bougainvillea spp. Bougainvillea
Distictis buccinatoria Blood-red trumpet vine
Hardenbergia spp. Lilac vine
Hedera spp. Ivy
Loniceria japonica Japanese honeysuckle
Passiflora spp. Passion vine
Rosa "Lady Banks' Lady Bank's rose
Solanum jasminoides Potato vine
Trachelospermum jasminoides Star jasmine

Succulents and Cacti

Aloe spp. Aloe
Calandrinia grandiflora, C. spectabilis Rock purslane
Cotyledon spp. Cotyledon
Crassula ovata Jade plant
Echeveria elegans Mexican snow ball
Dudleya spp. Liveforevers
Euphorbia spp. Euphorbia
Fouquieria splendens Ocotillo
Carpobrotus, Drosanthemum, Lampranthus Ice plant
Opuntia spp. Pancake cactus, Prickly pear
Sansevieria spp. Snake plant or Mother-In-law's tongue
Yucca spp. Yucca

Food Plants

Annuals: Artichoke, bush beans, cauliflower, cucumbers, peppers, tomatoes, zucchini

Berries: Blackberry, blueberry, raspberry, strawberry

Deciduous Fruit: Almond, fig, grape, plum, persimmon, walnut

Herbs: Comfrey, lemon balm, lavender, mint, rosemary, cooking sage

Tropical: Banana, cherimoya, date palm, guava, mango, passion fruit

Crops sensitive to salts: Avocados, citrus, various herbs, and seedlings

PART III

Plants

6

Grasses

Grasses are perennials with particular characteristics. They are monocots that have hollow stems, leaves that sheath, and flowers that are wind-pollinated. Grasses spread by seed, rhizomes (underground stems), stolons (above ground stems), and by clumping and expanding. Grasses can be spilt into two categories: cool and warm season.

Cool season grasses mostly come from mild winter areas, such as Southern California. They begin their growth with fall rains and usually go dormant in mid to late summer. While they like the soil dry in late summer and fall, they favor only slightly dry soil between winter and spring. Most can tolerate summer water, and may stay greener as a consequence, but they will rot if they get too much irrigation. Plant, divide and cut back these cool season growers between October and December.

Summer dormant, and winter and spring growing, red fescue is a cool season grass.

Warm season grasses mostly come from cold winter areas. They are winter dormant and wake up in spring, growing throughout summer. Between summer and fall, they should dry out only slightly between waterings, but winter through spring they require no irrigation. Plant, divide and cut back between January and March.

Winter dormant, and spring and summer growing, deer grass is a warm season grass.

General Growing Tips

Below are general guidelines for growing grasses and includes information on irrigation, fertilization, pruning and propagation. Following this section are specific recommendations for individual grasses.

Irrigation / Water Requirements

Generally, grasses are not the most drought tolerant plants. The showy, lush and big grasses that are sold at nurseries do not come from the deserts, but from the grasslands, plains, riparian, wetland and woodland environments, some of the least drought-stressed environments. The grasses listed below are at least semi-drought adapted. The more water-needy grasses, such as bog, moor and reed grasses, have been excluded for the most part.

Fertilizing / Fertilization

Most of the grasses sold at nurseries come from biologically rich areas with biologically complex soils. They favor fertile soils rich in both bacterial and fungal life. Mulch, compost and humus are all that is typically needed to keep them thriving. Some varieties, especially the larger grasses such as evergreen miscanthus, will require organic supplements high in nitrogen, such as manures and blood meal. However, a few of the grasses listed below are true savannah and scrub grasses and have adapted to poor, hardpan soils. Anything more than wood chips and mulch will hurt them. The needle grasses, melics and dropseed are good examples.

Pruning

Most grasses have adapted to some type of regular disturbance, whether flooding, grazing or wildfires. Therefore many grasses perform better with moderate levels of induced disturbance, whether that be mowing or shearing.

Mowing and shearing perennial grasses can be a grueling chore because leaves are fibrous and difficult to cut. The best tools are weed-whackers, hedge shears (not the powered trimmers) and hand pruning shears. Weed-whacking the larger grasses may require upgrading to a thicker string, or replacing string with a plastic or metal blade. Sharp blades are essential—using blunt blades is an exercise in futility.

Many ornamental grasses look better with periodic shearing. The *Carex tumulicola* pictured is cut back every other to every third year, keeping it green and flush with growth.

Propagation: Divisions

Clumping grasses produce new growth from their base and grow outward. They are easily divided and propagated. Commonly divided grasses include blue oat grass, deer grass, miscanthus and lyme grass.

As a Rule

1. If cool season, then begin division in late fall/early winter; if warm season, then begin late winter/early spring.

2. Start in cool weather.

3. Moisten soil to 1' deep: do not over saturate.

4. Dig up plants starting 4" to 6" from the plant's base.

5. If not dividing immediately, moisten, cover and shade the roots.

6. Cut the clump in halves or thirds using a sharp knife or pruning saw.

7. Plant the divisions immediately.

8. Moisten the soil to 1' deep.

9. If drainage is good, moisten soil up to twice a week; if not, no more than once a week.

10. Put on normal irrigation schedule in 4 weeks.

A clump of lemon grass (*Cymbopogon citratus*) dug up and cut in half.

Pests

Although grasses are one of the most problem-free plant palettes, they are not always pest-free. Aphids, gophers, mealybugs, rabbits, rot, rust, slugs, and snails are potential problems. Refer to the chapter on Natural Strategies for specifics on handling these pests. However, the best defense is always a strong offense:

Maintain Health for Pest Protection

▪ Do not overwater.

▪ Provide or ensure good drainage.

▪ Do not cut back out of season—it can take plants years to recover.

▪ Do not cut back too frequently; every other year is better than every year.

▪ Fertilize sparingly, relying mostly on wood chips, mulches and compost.

▪ Ensure air circulation.

Individual Plant Care

Grasses are usually known by their common names and that is how they are listed below. At the end of this chapter is a list of botanical names, and their common name equivalents.

Note: *Irrigation requirements are expressed in the amount of inches a soil should dry to before receiving supplemental water. Of course, if a soil never dries to prescribed depth, which is not uncommon, then the plant requires no irrigation.* ▪

Alkali Sacaton or Dropseed (*Sporobolus airoides*)
   Warm season. Southern California native. Tough. Can dry to 6" in spring and summer, to 1' in fall and winter. Dry to only 4" in spring in well draining soils. Suffers in wet, compacted soils. Prefers neutral to slightly alkaline soils. Low nutrient needs; yearly mulch only. Slow grower; no cutting or mowing is necessary.

Big bluestem (*Andtropogon gerardii*)
   Warm season. Tough. Can dry to 4". Needs no more than mulch and compost, although occasional organic supplements high in nitrogen may improve appearance. If rangy, mow to a couple of inches in winter (no later!). Divide and plant in winter. Corral where spreading rhizomes could be a problem. Does not tolerate shade.

Blue-eyed grass (*Sisyrinchium bellum*)
Refer to the section on Low Growing and Rooting Perennials in the Perennial chapter.

Blue grama (*Bouteloua gracilis*)
Warm season. This grass is drought adapted and with roots that grow to 2' it can dry to 6" to 9". If rangy or listless, mow to ground in fall. Low nutrient needs; a little mulch and bare soil are all that it needs. If walked on, then aeration may be required. May need corralling. Its seeds are slow to spread, which means being careful not to trample seedlings.

Blue oat grass (*Helictotrichon sempervirens*)
Cool season. Along the coast, in the shade, and in cool environments let the soil dry to 6", in hot dry areas to 4". Suffers from rot and rust in wet soils or humid environments. Moderate feeder that needs compost, humus, and occasional well-balanced organic fertilizer. If untidy, mow to 3" in fall. Plant in fall and early winter.

Buffalo grass (*Buchloe dactyloides*)
Warm season. Tough lawn substitute. Can dry to 4". Low nutrient needs; mulches and compost are sufficient. Occasionally requires aeration. Can be treated as a lawn replacement and mowed but is rarely mowed when used as a meadow grass. It runs and may need corralling. Slow to establish and fertilizers won't help.

Bunch cutgrass (*Leersia monandra*)
Cool season. Dry to 2" in sun, 6" in shade. Prefers neutral pH and low nutrients; mulch and compost are all that are necessary. The grass can be mowed to improve appearance in fall. Plant in fall and winter.

California oatgrass (*Danthonia californica*)
Cool season. A Southern California native. Dry to no more than 4" in spring and fall, but can tolerate up to 6" in summer (although it stays green with regular summer irrigation). Nutrients needs are moderately low; mulch and compost are sufficient. Can reseed and regenerate. If untidy, mow in fall. Plant or sow in late fall, early winter.

Cane bluestem (*Bothriochloa barbinodis*)
Warm season. Southern California native. Tough. Along the coast dries to 6" in winter and spring, and up to 9" in summer and fall. Inland it dries to 6" year round. Low nutrient needs; nothing more than a light layer of wood chips or mulch is needed. Deadhead late fall. If looking rangy or tired, mow to 4" in late winter/early spring. Plant in winter and spring.

Deer grass (*Muhlenbergia rigens*)
Warm season. Southern California native found in protected or moist locations. For best appearance dry to 4" in spring and 6" in summer and fall. No irrigation in winter. Low nutrient needs; mulch and compost will do. Deadhead in early winter. If rangy or tired looking, cut back to 6" late fall to early spring. Divide and plant in winter and spring.

Evergreeen miscanthus (*Miscanthus transmorrisonensis*)
Warm season. While it is hardy and dries to 6" year round, because of the size of this grass, the soil around it tends to dry out quickly. Therefore it will need more frequent irrigation. Preferring fertile soils, it requires mulch or compost plus organic supplements high in nitrogen. Remove dead leaves and deadhead in winter. Divide and plant in late winter/early spring.

Fescue, blue (*Festuca glauca*)
Cool season. Likes to be moderately dry between waterings. Dry to 3" inland and 6" along the coast. Not big feeders; mulches and compost are sufficient. Deadhead late summer if desired. Rarely needs cutting back. The centers will begin to die in older clumps and replanting will be necessary. They are prone to rot in hot and humid environments.

Fescue, California (*Festuca californica*)
Cool season. California native. Dry to 4" in full sun in winter and spring, 6" to 9" in summer and fall. Right along the coast and in the shade dry to 6" in winter and spring, and give no irrigation the rest of the year. Moderately low nutrients requirements; mulch or compost will suffice. Deadhead late summer. If untidy, them either rake out dead leaves or cut two-thirds off the top in late fall. Plant in late fall and winter.

Fescue, creeping red (*Festuca rubra*)
Cool season. California native. If in a cool coastal or shaded area, dry to 4" to 6", but if inland and hot, then dry to only 3". Will suffer with too much water. Prefers slightly acidic soils with low to moderate nutrients, rarely needing more than a dose of blood meal in fall. It spreads by rhizomes, but seldom needs corralling. Rake out dead material between late fall and late winter.

Fountain grass, Bunny tail (*Pennisetum messiacum 'Bunny Tails'*)
Warm season. Dry to 4" year round for best appearance. Prefers fertile soils; yearly compost should do, although a well-balanced organic fertilizer may be needed occasionally. Deadhead in late fall. If rangy looking, cut to 4" in early spring. Plant in winter and spring.

Fountain grass, red (*Pennisetum x advena 'Rubrum'*)
Warm season. Dry adapted and looks good year round if soil dries to 4" to 6", depending on distance from coast. Too much water creates leggy, lanky growth. Moderate nutrients needs; nothing more than mulch, compost or humus is needed. Deadhead early fall. Divide if necessary in late winter. Mow grass to 4"-6" early spring if looking untidy. Can rot in wet, compacted soils.

Hairgrass (*Deschampsia* spp.)
Cool season. Only moderately drought tolerant. Dry to 3" in sun, to 5" in the shade. Suffers in hot and dry situations. Prefers slightly acidic, rich soil. Moderate feeders; compost, humus and organics may be needed regularly. Divide and cut back in fall. Plant in late winter/early spring.

June grass (*Koeleria macrantha*)
Cool season. California native. Drought resilient. Prefers 6" dry year round. Low nutrient needs; mulch only. Suffer in wet and compacted conditions. Slow grower and so it should be encouraged to seed. Deadhead in early fall. Plant in late winter. It is an allergen.

Lemon grass (*Cymbopogon citratus*)
Warm season. Dry to 4" in full sun, to 6" in the shade, year round. Moderate feeder; will need organic additives if not planted in fertile soil. Divide and cut back in winter/early spring. Frost sensitive (the leaves will look burned if affected).

Melic, California (*Melica californica*)
Cool season. Southern California native. Hardy and can dry to 6" year round. Requires almost no supplemental water in shade. Low nutrient needs; wood chips or mulch are sufficient. Mow in fall if looking rangy or tired. Sow seeds in fall through winter. Will suffer in wet, compacted conditions.

Melic, coastal range (*Melica imperfecta*)
Cool season. Southern California native. Can dry to 6" year round. May need no irrigation in shade. Prefers neutral pH and low nutrients; mulch or compost only. If looking rangy, mow in fall. Sow seeds in fall and winter.

Mexican feather grass (*Stipa tenuissima (Nassella tenuissima)*)
Cool Season. Mexican feather grass is an aggressive invasive plant and it should not be planted. It easily self-sows and mowing the top 6" in late spring before the grass sets seed will help control its spread.

Muhly, bamboo (*Muhlenbergia dumosa*)
Warm season. Drought tolerant and can dry 4" to 6" in summer, although it is more attractive if soils only dry to 2" winter and spring. Prefers fertile soils; mulch, compost or humus with occasional organic additives may be required. Remove dead stems, deadhead and thin in early winter. Divide and plant in late winter/early spring.

Muhly, pink or Hairawn muhly (*Muhlenbergia capillaris*)
Warm season. Drought adapted. Dry to 4" to 6" year round, depending on distance from coast. Moderate nutrient needs; compost or humus will suffice. Deadhead in early winter. Divide and plant in late winter. Some plants will lose the pink of their blooms and have to be replaced.

Needlegrass—nodding, foothill and purple (*Stipa (Nassella) cernua,*
S. lepida, S. pulchra)
Cool season. California natives. Exceptionally drought adapted. Dry to 6" fall through spring. No irrigation late summer/early fall (it is dormant). Suffers from too much water and/or compaction. Low nutrient needs; nothing more than mulch is needed. Mow in late summer/fall. Plant and seed in fall/early winter.

Purple three-awn (*Aristida purpurea*)
Warm season. Southern California native. Drought adapted. Dry to 5" or 9" year round, depending on distance from coast. Low nutrient needs; slow to decompose wood chips and mulch only. The sharp-barbed awns can be a public/pet nuisance and the seeds are fertile, meaning that it should be sheared/mowed before it sets its awns in summer. If regeneration is desired, mow it in fall.

Reed grass, Mendocino (*Calamagrostis foliosa*)
Cool season. Dry soil to 4" along the coast, only 2" inland. Low to moderate nutrient needs; mulch and compost is usually all that is needed. Deadhead in late summer. If looking untidy, then cut top one-third of grass in fall. Plant in fall.

Ruby grass (*Melinis nerviglumis*)
Warm season. Drought resilient. Dry to 4" in spring and then to 6" the rest of the year. Moderate feeder; nothing more than compost or humus is required. Deadhead in winter. Cut back to a couple inches in spring if damaged from frost. Plant in late winter/early spring.

Rye, blue or Blue lyme grass (*Leymus arenarius* 'Glaucus')
Cool season. Dry to 2" in spring and fall, to 4" in summer. Moderate feeder; nothing more than yearly compost or humus is needed. Thin, divide and plant in fall. If untidy, cut back to only a couple inches in fall. If propagating, divide in fall. Aggressive spreader in moist airy environments and will need corralling.

Rye, Canyon prince wild (*Elymus condensatus* 'Canyon Prince')
Cool season. California native. As a riparian it needs moisture spring and fall, drying to 2", but can take considerable dryness in summer, drying to 6". Moderate nutrient needs; mulch, compost and humus should do. Plant and divide in fall. Mow to a couple inches any time if looking rangy or untidy.

Rye, great basin wild (*Elymus cinereus*)
Cool season. California native. Prefers to be only slightly dry (to 2") in fall and spring but can tolerate to 6" in summer. Moderate feeder; mulch and compost will suffice, although a complete organic fertilizer will be needed if in poor coarse soil. If looking rangy, cut back to a couple inches in fall. Plant fall and winter.

Rye, wild blue (*Elymus glaucus*)
Cool season. A California native. Grows best with moisture; dry to only 3" in the sun, 4" in shade. Prefers neutral pH and a little nutrients; mulch and compost should suffice. Short lived and can reseed itself; mow after the grass has set seed.

Sedge, dune, San Diego and Berkeley (*Carex pansa C. spissa*, *C. tumulicola*)
Not a grass, but a sedge. Most sedges are cool season plants and will stay green with moisture and warm temperatures. Dry to 2" or 4" for best appearance. These sedges prefer slightly acidic soils and are quick to show signs of nitrogen deficiencies, indicating they need humus or organic additives high in nitrogen. Deadhead in summer by weed whacking. If looking untidy, mow to a couple inches in late fall/early winter. Plant in winter. C. *pansa* may need corralling.

Switch grass (*Panicum virgatum*)
Warm season. Includes many cultivars. Can become drought resilient and thrive in soils dried to 6" in the summer and fall. For best appearance dry to only 2" in late spring. Deadhead in fall. Low nutrient needs; mulch and compost only. If rangy, shear to 4" to 6" in late winter/spring. Plant in late winter/ spring. Moist conditions can cause problems and the grass can send out rhizomes, self-sow and get rust in damp conditions.

Zoysia or Korean velvetgrass (*Zoysia* spp.)
Warm season. Dries to 3" throughout the year. Low nitrogen needs for a lawn alternative, but it still requires 2 to 3 pounds of nitrogen a year (per 1,000sf). Because of zoysia's dense mat-like growth, mulches and composts are more detrimental than beneficial. Organic fertilizers such as blood meal, activated sludge and distilled manures are best and need to be washed in. If looking tired, mow to 1" and apply compost and humus in late winter/early spring.

Botanical Names to Common

Andtropogon gerardii Big bluestem
Aristida purpurea Purple three-awn
Bothriochloa barbinodis Cane bluestem
Bouteloua gracilis Blue grama
Buchloe dactyloides Buffalo grass
Calamagrostis foliosa Mendocino reed grass
Carex pansa C. spissa, C. tumulicola Sedge, dune, San Diego and Berkeley
Cymbopogon citratus Lemon grass
Danthonia californica California oatgrass
Deschampsia spp. Hairgrass
Elymus cinereus Great basin wild rye
Elymus condensatus 'Canyon Prince' Canyon prince wild rye
Elymus glaucus Wild Blue Rye
Festuca californica California fescue
Festuca glauca Blue fescue
Festuca rubra Creeping Red fescue
Helictotrichon sempervirens Blue oat grass
Koeleria macrantha June grass
Leersia monandra Bunch cutgrass
Leymus arenarius 'Glaucus' Blue rye or Blue lyme grass

Melica californica California melic
Melica imperfecta Coastal range melic
Melinis nerviglumis Ruby grass
Miscanthus transmorrisonensis Evergreeen miscanthus
Muhlenbergia capillaris Pink muhly or Hairawn muhly
Muhlenbergia dumosa Bamboo muhly
Muhlenbergia rigens Deer grass
Panicum virgatum Switch grass
Pennisetum x advena 'Rubrum' Red fountain grass
Pennisetum messiacum 'Bunny Tails' Bunny tail fountain grass
Sporobolus airoides Alkali Sacaton or Dropseed
Stipa (Nassella) cernua, N. lepida, N. pulchra Needlegrass—nodding, foothill and purple
Stipa tenuissima (Nassella tenuissima) Mexican feather grass
Zoysia spp. Zoysia or Korean Velvetgrass

Common Names to Botantical

Alkali sacaton or Dropseed *Sporobolus airoides*
Big bluestem *Andtropogon gerardii*
Blue grama *Bouteloua gracilis*
Blue oat grass *Helictotrichon sempervirens*
Buffalo grass *Buchloe dactyloides*
Bunch cutgrass *Leersia monandra*
California oatgrass *Danthonia californica*
Cane bluestem *Bothriochloa barbinodis*
Deer grass *Muhlenbergia rigens*
Evergreeen miscanthus *Miscanthus transmorrisonensis*
Fescue, blue *Festuca glauca*
Fescue, California *Festuca californica*
Fescue, creeping red *Festuca rubra*
Fountain grass, Bunny tail *Pennisetum messiacum* 'Bunny Tails'
Fountain grass, red *Pennisetum x advena* 'Rubrum'
Hairgrass *Deschampsia* spp.
June grass *Koeleria macrantha*
Lemon grass *Cymbopogon citratus*
Melic, California *Melica californica*
Melic, coastal range *Melica imperfecta*
Mexican feather grass *Stipa tenuissima (Nassella tenuissima)*
Muhly, bamboo *Muhlenbergia dumosa*

Muhly, pink or Hairawn muhly *Muhlenbergia capillaris*

Needlegrass—Nodding, foothill and purple *Stipa (Nassella) cernua, N. lepida, N. pulchra*

Purple three-awn *Aristida purpurea*

Reed grass, Mendocino *Calamagrostis foliosa*

Ruby grass *Melinis nerviglumis*

Rye, blue or blue lyme grass *Leymus arenarius* 'Glaucus'

Rye, canyon prince wild *Elymus condensatus* 'Canyon Prince'

Rye, great basin wild *Elymus cinereus*

Rye, wild blue *Elymus glaucus*

Sedge, dune, San Diego and Berkeley *Carex pansa C. spissa, C. tumulicola*

Switch grass *Panicum virgatum*

Zoysia or Korean velvetgrass *Zoysia* spp.

7

Perennials

Perennials are one of the most neighborly plant groups. They live within nearly every plant community. They help landscapes recover from fire or flood. And they are committed to community connections—they evolve soil complexity, birds and bugs devour their seeds, and 95% are animal pollinated, supporting bees, butterflies and many other important pollinators.

Perennials provide connections and cheer. Technically, a perennial is any dicot that lives longer than two years (grasses are monocots). However, that distinction includes shrubs and trees, which most of us don't think of as perennials. More precisely defined, a perennial is herbaceous, which means its stems are non-woody. Some perennials, such as bulbs, dieback each year; some, such as buckwheat, go dormant in either winter or summer; and some—*Dymondia*, for instance—grow nearly all year. This chapter also includes some plants that are considered sub-shrubs; the plants like lavender that sit between perennials and shrubs.

This chapter provides general growing tips followed by specific recommendations for both low-growing rooting perennials and the larger varieties.

The perennial gardens at Camrosa Water District, Camarillo.

General Growing Tips

Below are general guidelines for growing perennials and includes information on irrigation, soils, fertilization, pruning and propagation. Following this section are specific recommendations for individual perennials.

Irrigation / Water Requirements

Irrigation for low-growing, rooting perennials is typically different than for the larger perennials. The low growers are commonly used because they are aggressive enough to choke out weeds: in essence, they become the weed. To get the density necessary to be an effective weed block, these perennials need overhead sprinklers. An even distribution of moisture allows for a greater distribution of rooting. Also, unlike most of the other plants in this book, these low growers should get water at a greater frequency, but for a much shorter duration.

The larger perennials are better suited to low-flow and spot irrigation. In fact, overhead irrigation increases chances of rot and pest problems for many of these plants.

Soil and Fertilization

The perennials listed in this chapter come from many different Mediterranean environments including fire-scarred, scrubland, desert, savannah, meadow, streamside, floodplains, and woodland understory. Therefore sweeping recommendations are problematic. However, there are general differences between the two groups presented below.

Low-Growing Rooting Perennials: Most of the plants in this list are either streamside or woodland perennials; there are few desert perennials in this category. Aggressive ground covers come from environments with more water and nutrients. Generally, this group favors light but more frequent watering, soil with neutral to slightly acidic pH, and low to moderate amounts of organic matter and nutrients. Fertilization may be needed because wood chips, mulch and compost can smother these low growers. Good all-purpose organic fertilizers include activated sludge, manures, and animal meals, such as blood and bone meal.

In the right conditions yarrow (*Achillea* spp.) will take over. It spreads by both underground stems and seed.

Larger Perennials: This is a tougher bunch and desert and scrub perennials are better represented. Generally, many of these plants (but not all) favor a soak and dry cycle of irrigation, neutral pH (with many tolerating slightly alkaline) and low levels of nutrients. Wood chips, mulches, and compost are all that is needed. These perennials are more prone to rot than the low growers.

This beautiful garden is awash in large perennials—Mexican bush sage, Mexican lobelia, rosemary and Santa Barbara daisy flourish.

The recommendations below represent the environment from which they evolved.

Pruning

Low growing rooting perennials can be maintained with a variety of approaches. Mowing, pinching, shearing, thinning and weed whacking can all be used. Some of these plants get cut nearly to the ground, while others are rarely touched.

The larger perennials may need to be lightly sheared for compactness or containment, selectively thinned for aesthetics and health, or both.

As a Rule

- Avoid pruning out of season; it increases chances of climatic injury and pest infestations.

- Never prune when the soil is wet or soggy. Soil compaction is the result, which creates a slew of ill effects. Any work should occur when the soil is dry, or just slightly moist.

Propagation

Perennials are generally easy to propagate. Both their vegetative parts and seeds are eager to root.

Plants in the low-growing rooting perennial section propagate readily from above ground stems (stolons) and/or underground shoots (rhizomes), both of which can be cut off the plant and planted elsewhere. The larger perennials can be started by 5" stem cuttings from the growing ends. These cuttings can either be put in a glass with a couple inches of water, a proper rooting medium, or planted directly into the ground, although the later has the lowest success rate. Some of these larger plants also produce root offshoots, which can be cut from the plant.

Coral bells are notorious spreaders and easily propagated by digging out and dividing the young starts.

Individual Plant Care

The plants below are listed by their botanic names. They are also cross-listed by their common names at the end of the chapter.

Note: *Irrigation requirements are expressed in the amount of inches a soil should dry before receiving supplemental water. Of course, if a soil never dries to prescribed depth, which is not uncommon during monsoons, then the plant requires no irrigation.* ■

Low Growing and Rooting Perennials

Achillea spp. Yarrow
Meadow natives from Southern California. Can dry to 4" spring and summer, 6" in fall. No irrigation in winter. Low nutrient needs and nothing more than wood chips, mulch or compost is required. Deadhead in fall. Divide, seed and plant late fall/ early winter.

Armeria spp. Sea pink or Thrift
Coastal plant. Dry to 4" to 5" between watering in spring through fall, but only to 2" to 3" inland. Dry to 6" in winter. Low nutrient needs; wood chips and mulch may be occasionally needed in late winter/early spring. Drainage is essential. Rots in dense, fertile or moist soils. Deadhead in late summer. Divide and plant late winter/spring.

Aurina saxatile Basket of gold
Dry to 4" year around. Prone to rot in moist dense soils. Low nutrient needs and mulch and compost will do. If looking rangy, then cut the plant in half in late fall. Plant in late fall/winter.

Calylophus berlandieri, C. hartwegii Sundrops
Favors dry conditions and can dry to 6" along coast and 4" inland spring and summer, dry to a 1' in fall. No irrigation in winter. Moderate nutrient needs but the plant blooms a little better if a light (reduce strength by ¼), well-balanced fertilizer is given late winter every year. If rangy, cut or mow to a couple inches in late winter/ early spring.

Ceratostigma plumbaginoides Dwarf plumbago

Dry to 4" in sandy soils (its preference) and to 6" in clay. Low nutrient needs; wood chips, mulch, or compost is all that is needed. If looking lackluster, then a light, well-balanced fertilizer late winter will help. Mowing or shearing every other year can increase vigor and regeneration from rhizomes. Propagate by pushing stems into the soil in late fall/winter. Plant in late winter/spring.

Chamaemelum nobile Chamomile

Tough plant. Can dry to 4" spring and early summer, 6" in fall. No irrigation in winter. In dense, heavy soils dry to 6" in spring and summer. Low nutrient needs; nothing more than wood chips and mulch is required. Propagate from cuttings in winter. Push rooting stems into ground and plant in late winter/spring. Seed in fall.

Clinopodium (Satureja) douglasii Yerba buena (Yerba yuena)

Californian coastal native. Fog-adapted, it looks best if it does not dry to more than 4" year round. Moderate nutrient needs; as well as yearly compost, it may require organic supplements, especially if grown in poor soil. If rangy looking, mow or shear in late winter/early spring. Pinch or lightly shear to induce bushiness. Easy to propagate by stem cuttings.

Convolvulus mauritanicus, C. sabatius Ground morning glory

Dry to 5" along coast; 3" to 4" inland. Suffers from overwatering in clay soils. Low to moderate nutrient needs; compost and a well-balanced organic fertilizer may be needed every other year. If looking rangy, thin and shear to 3" in late winter. Seed and plant late winter/ early spring.

Coreopsis auriculata 'Nana' Tickseed

Dry to 4" in spring, 6" in summer and fall. No irrigation in winter. Low to moderate nutrient needs; mulch and compost will do. Deadhead by shearing in mid-summer. Taking cuttings, seed and plant late winter/spring. Sometimes short-lived.

Duchesnea indica Indian mock strawberry

Grows best with regular water. Dry to only 3" in spring and summer, 6" in fall and winter. Moderate feeder and compost or a yearly application of a well-balanced fertilizer may be needed. If looking rangy or weedy looking, mow to 2". Take root cuttings and/or plant in late winter/early spring.

Dymondia margaretae Dymondia
Although it tolerates drought, dymondia grows best and out com-
petes weeds if only slightly dry between watering; dry to 3" in
spring and summer, 5" in fall. No irrigation in winter. Low nutrient
needs, but because of its tight-matting nature, fertilize every year
with a light, well-balanced organic supplement late winter/early
spring. Plant root offsets in late winter/early spring.

Erigeron karvinskianus Mexican daisy or Santa Barbara daisy
Drought and fire-adapted. Let dry to 4" in spring, 6" in summer and
fall. No irrigation in winter. Low to moderate nutrient needs; mulch,
compost and an occasional organic supplement will be needed. To
encourage rich new growth, mow nearly to the ground in winter/
early spring at a minimum of every other year.

Erigeron glaucus Seaside daisy
California coastal plant that looks better if it never dries to more
than 4" spring and summer, 6" in fall. No irrigation in winter. Moderate nutrient needs; compost and an occasional organic supplement
will be necessary. If looking listless, ratty or pest-infested, cut back
to a couple inches above soil in late fall and mulch. Individual plants
may not be long-lived, but they do spread and seed.

Fragaria chiloensis, F. vesca (californica) Wild strawberry, Sand strawberry
For densest cover, do not dry to more than 4" along the coast,
2" inland, spring through fall. No irrigation in winter. Moderate
nutrient needs. Because of its dense, matting nature, well-balanced
organic fertilizers will be required; early spring is the best time
to apply. If rangy or listless, mow and rake out dead foliage in late
winter. Divide and plant in late winter/early spring. *F. vesca* is better
in dense soils.

Gazania hybrids Gazania
Dry to 4" along the coast spring through fall; no irrigation in winter. In the hotter, drier areas gazania looks better if only dried to
2" to 4" year round. Moderate feeders; compost is recommended
yearly, organic supplements every other year. Clumps or patches will
occasionally die off; plan on replanting every 2 or 3 years.

Grindelia hirsutula gumplant
Coastal native in Southern California and cool season grower. Dry to
only 4" in winter and spring, but up to 9" in summer and fall. May
require more irrigation in coarse or sandy soils. Low nutrient needs;
wood chips and mulch is all that is needed. Take cuttings in winter.
Plant in late fall/winter.

Helichryum spp. Curry and Licorice plants
Dry to 4" spring and summer, 6" in fall. No irrigation in winter. Too much water and fertilizer will shorten this plant's life. Leaves laying on moist soil will rot. Low nutrient needs; mulch and compost will do. Regular pinching will help maintain strong form. Push stems into ground to root in winter. Plant in late fall and winter.

Herniaria glabra Rupture wort
Dry to only 4" year around. Moderate nutrient needs; well-balanced organic concentrates will be needed yearly. Push stems into soil to root and plant late winter/spring.

Heuchera spp. Coral bells or Alum root
Some Southern California natives. Winter dormant. Dry to just 4" spring, 6" in summer and fall. No irrigation in winter. Moderate nutrient needs. Apply mulch or compost yearly. If the plants become too dense and mulches become infeasible, use a light well-balanced organic supplement. Propagate and plant in early spring. Prone to mites in dry, dusty environments; wash foliage yearly to prevent an infestation.

Lessingia filaginifolia '*Silver Carpet*' California beach aster or Sand aster
California native and summer dormant. Dry to 4" in late winter and spring, to 8" in summer and early fall. Dries to a 1' in the shade. Low nutrient needs; wood chips and mulch will do. Too much moisture and nutrients will shorten its life. Propagate by pushing stems into moist soil late fall and winter. Plant in late fall/winter. Little care needed along coast.

Malvastrum lateritium Trailing mallow
Tough and durable. Dry to 6" in spring, 9" in summer, and just 4" in late fall and winter. Low nutrient needs; mulch and compost are sufficient. If looking rangy, mow or shear to 2" late fall/early winter. Stems root easily; cut and push them into the soil in winter.

Matricaria recutita German chamomile
A summer grower. Prefers only drying to 4" in spring and summer, but can dry to 6" in fall. No irrigation in winter. Low to moderate nutrient needs; mulch and compost usually suffice. The plant may struggle in dense clay soils. Take stem cuttings in winter, plant early spring. Sow seeds collected in fall in late winter/spring. This chamomile is said to be sweeter than *Chamaemelum nobile*.

Mentha x piperita, M. spicata Peppermint and Spearmint
Can dry to 6" in considerable shade, but no less than 4" year round if in full sun. Likes fertile acidic soils, and mulch, compost and humus are all that is needed. Pinch or shear to induce bushiness in late winter/early spring. If rangy looking, mow or shear to 2" in winter. Propagate stems by pushing them into the ground in winter. Prone to mites in dry dusty environments; washing the foliage yearly helps.

Monardella villosa Coyote mint
Native to the northern parts of the state. Dry to 6" year around. Low to moderate nutrient needs; wood chips or mulch and occasionally humus will suffice. If looking rangy, shear the top two-thirds in late winter/early spring. Propagate by pushing stems in soil in late winter/early spring.

Nepeta cataria Catnip
Dry to 3" in sandy soils, but up to 6" in clay soils in spring through fall. No irrigation in winter. Moderate nutrient needs; yearly compost plus an occasional well-balanced organic supplement will improve appearance. If rangy looking, mow or shear to 2" in late winter/early spring.

Oenothera elata hookeri Hooker's evening primrose
Southern California native with its home in areas of seasonal flooding. Prefers a wet winter and spring, drying to only 3", and a dry summer and fall, drying to 6" or more. Moderate nutrient needs. In average soil yearly wood chips and mulch should be sufficient; in sandy soil, a well-balanced organic supplement may be required as well. Do not deadhead until late fall to ensure seed dispersal. Divide and plant in late fall/early winter.

Origanum majorana, O. vulgare Sweet marjoram, Oregano
Tough, but needs a wet spring and early summer, drying to only 4". Can dry to 6" in fall. No irrigation in winter. Low nutrient needs; wood chips, mulch and compost will suffice. Will rot in dense clay and moist soils. If looking rangy, shear or mow to 3" in late winter/early spring. Propagates easily from divisions and stem cuttings in winter.

Osteospermum fruticosum African daisy, Freeway daisy
Drought-adapted, but it looks better if irrigated. Dry to 4"–6" throughout the year, depending on distance from coast. Moderate nutrient needs; well-balanced organic supplements, even chemical fertilizers, may be needed yearly. Pinch or lightly shear growing tips to encourage compactness. If looking rangy or twiggy, mow to 4" in late fall/early winter.

***Pelargonium* spp.** Common geranium, Ivy geranium, Martha Washington
Dry to 4" in spring and summer, 6" in fall and winter. Moderate nutrient needs; well-balanced organic fertilizers should be given yearly. Pinch or shear to induce bushiness. Propagate by cuttings in winter. Prone to all types of biting/sucking insects. Keeping the area dry and using companion plants helps reduce infestations.

Phyla nodiflora Lippia
Southern California native found along and near streams and wetlands. Prefers drying to no more than 4" in winter and spring, no more than 6" in summer and fall. Low to moderate nutrient needs, but because of its matting nature, light well-balanced organic supplements may be needed every other year. Might suffer in dense soils. Mow or shear rangy twiggy growth late winter/spring. Push stems in soil to propagate in winter/spring. Prone to nematodes.

***Potentilla* spp.** Potentilla or Cinquefoil
Many Southern California natives. They are found mostly along streams and wetlands. Dry to 4" year round. Moderate nutrient needs; compost and well-balanced organic fertilizers may be needed yearly. It favors good drainage and aeration may be necessary if in area with foot traffic or where soil has been compacted. Mow or shear yearly in late winter/early spring to remove rangy, twiggy growth. Propagation is easy with stem cuttings and root divisions in winter/spring.

Salvia chamaedryoides Germander sage
Dry to only 6" winter and spring, but 9" in summer and 1' in fall. Low nutrient needs; wood chips and mulch will suffice. Favors well draining soils and suffers in clay, especially if wet. Deadhead late fall. Easy to spread by pushing stems into ground in winter. Plant in late winter/spring.

Salvia sinaloensis Sinaloa sage

Dry to 4" in spring, 6" in summer, 9" in fall. No irrigation in winter. Moderate nutrient needs; as well as compost, a mild well-balanced organic supplement may also needed. It prefers coarse soils—clay soils with moisture may kill it. If looking rangy, mow or shear to 3" late winter/early spring. Propagates easily by pushing stems into ground in late winter/early spring.

Salvia sonomensis Sonoma sage

California native. Dry to only 6" in winter and spring, 9" in summer and fall. Low nutrient needs; wood chips, mulch or compost may be needed yearly. Favors shade and struggles in sun, especially inland. If looking rangy, mow or shear to 2" late fall/early winter. Easy to propagate by pushing the stems into soil in winter.

Sidalcea malviflora Checkerbloom or Prairie mallow

Coastal/near coastal Southern California native. Favors a wet winter and spring. Dry to just 4" during that period but can dry to 6" to 9" in summer and fall depending on distance from coast. Low nutrient needs; wood chips, mulch or compost is all that are required. Deadhead after the seeds have set in summer. Propagates easily from rooting stems in winter/spring.

Sisyrinchium bellum Blue-eyed grass

Despite its common name, this is not a true grass. Native to the canyons and crevices of Southern California. Treat as a warm season grower. Dry to 3" to 6" in spring through fall. No irrigation in winter. Needs much less irrigation in shade. Low to moderate nutrient needs; nothing more than mulch, compost or humus required. Since it is a slow spreader seedlings should be encouraged; deadhead in late summer after seeds have matured. Plant late winter/early spring. Propagate by division and seed.

Stachys byzantina Lamb's ears

Dry to 4" in spring through fall. No irrigation in winter. Moderate nutrient needs; while wood chips and mulch are best, organic supplements may be needed because of its matting nature. The plant will rot with too much moisture, humidity and overhead irrigation. Remove dead leaves and stems year round. Vigorously thin in late winter/spring to invigorate. Propagates easily from stem cuttings in spring.

Stachys bullata Hedge nettle

Southern California native. In full sun dry to 5" spring/summer, 9" in fall. No irrigation in winter. In the shade, dry to 9" late winter/ spring. No irrigation fall/winter. Low to moderate nutrient needs; yearly mulch and compost may be needed. If looking rangy, mow or shear to 4" late winter/early spring. Spreads by rhizomes and easy to propagate and plant in spring.

Symphyotrichum chilense California aster

Southern California native. Dry to 4" spring and summer, 6" in fall. No irrigation in winter. Low nutrient needs; yearly light application of wood chips or mulch is all that is needed. Weed whack in fall if looking rangy. Propagate and plant in late winter/spring. Favors clay soils.

Teucrium cossonii Majorcan, Teucrium or Fruity germander

Dry to 4" in spring, 6" to 8" in summer and fall. No irrigation in winter. Low to moderate nutrient needs; mulch and compost will do. Will rot in dense, moist soils. If rangy looking, mow or shear to 2" to 3" in late winter/early spring. Propagate by pushing stems into soil in spring.

Thyme spp. Thyme (the creeping varieties)

Dry to 4" year-round inland, 4" to 6" along the coast. Moderate nutrient needs; a mild well-balanced organic supplement may be needed because mulch and compost smothers the plant. Will suffer in dense, wet soils. If rangy, mow or shear to 1" to 2" late winter/ spring. Propagate by stem cuttings in late winter through spring.

Tradescantia pallida, P. spathacea Purple heart, Moses in the cradle

Looks best if it never dries more than 4" to 6" year round. Moderate feeder; mulch or compost will be needed yearly, plus an occasional mild organic fertilizer low in nitrogen. Pinch or shear P. *pallida* for compactness. Propagate from stem cuttings in spring.

Trifolium spp. Clover

This Genus includes both Southern California natives and invasive weeds. Dry to only 4" in late winter through early summer, then 6" in summer through fall. No irrigation in late fall/early winter. Though it is a nitrogen fixer that needs little nutrients once established, a mild organic supplement can improve appearance. If rangy, mow or shear to 1" to 2" late winter/early spring.

Tropaeolum spp. Nasturtium

Dry to only 4" in spring, 6" in summer and fall. No irrigation in winter. Low to moderate nutrient needs. Since it is difficult to mulch and compost, a mild organic fertilizer may be needed every other year for best appearance. Favors sandy soils. If looking rangy, mow or shear to 4" in late winter/early spring. Collect seeds late spring and sow in winter through early spring.

Verbena peruviana, V. pulchella gracilior, V. tenuisecta Verbena, Moss verbena

Dry to 4" in spring, 6" in summer and fall. No irrigation in winter. Low nutrient needs; mulch and compost will suffice. Will rot in dense wet soils and/or wet, humid conditions. Pinch or lightly shear in early spring to induce bushiness. Easy to propagate from stem cuttings; push them into the ground in late winter through early spring.

Veronica liwanensis, V. repens Turkish speedwell, Creeping speedwell

Dry to 4" in late winter and early spring, and 6" the rest of the year. Low to moderate nutrient needs; usually nothing more than mulch and compost is necessary. Dry between waterings. Pinch or shear to induce bushiness in late winter/early spring. Propagates easily from stem cuttings in winter and spring.

Individual Plant Care: Larger Perennials

Agapanthus africanus, A. orientalis Lily of the Nile

Dry to 9" spring/summer and to 1' fall/winter along the coast; but inland dry to 6" in spring/summer, 9" in fall/winter. Low nutrient needs; a regular layer of mulch or compost will do. Deadheading in late summer and removing dead leaves are the only maintenance tasks.

Anigozanthos spp. Kangaroo paws

Dry to only 4" to 6" in spring through fall. No irrigation in winter. Moderate nutrient needs; an organic supplement low in phosphorus will be needed every spring. Prefers good drainage and will rot with too much moisture. Deadheading and removing dead leaves are the only pruning tasks.

Artemisia douglasiana California mugwort

Southern California native found along the scoured banks of rivers, creeks and flood plains. Dry to 6" throughout the year. Low nutrient needs; wood chips and mulch will suffice. Favors coarser soils. Deadhead after the summer flowers have set seed in fall. If rangy or twiggy, mow or shear to 4" in winter. Spreads by rhizomes and is easily propagated by root divisions in spring.

Artemisia schmidtiana Angel's hair

Dry to 6" in spring/fall, 4" in summer. No irrigation in winter. Requires almost no irrigation in the shade along the coast. Can rot with too much moisture. Modest nutrient needs; besides a layer of wood chips, a light well-balanced organic supplement may be needed every year in early spring. Pinch and lightly shear to maintain compactness. Does not respond well to pruning. Might be short-lived.

***Asclepias* spp.** Milkweed

Includes some California natives (but these are harder to find). Along the coast dry to 4" to 6" spring through fall. No irrigation in winter. Inland dry to only 3" to 4", 6" in winter. Low to moderate nutrient needs; mulch, compost and a light well-balanced organic supplement may improve appearance. Apply mulch in fall, organic supplements in late winter/spring. Cut nearly to ground in late fall if looking rangy. Taking cuttings of plant and root in spring. Plant in winter through spring. Readily reseeds itself if allowed. Importantly, do not be worried about insect damage—the caterpillar of the Monarch devours the plant.

***Coleonema* spp.** Breath of heaven

Dry to 4" along coast, 2" to 3" inland, in spring through fall. No irrigation in winter. Low nutrient needs; nothing more than a light layer of compost is needed yearly. Deadhead late spring. Thin and shear plant in late winter/early spring to induce bushiness and encourage spread by rhizomes.

Cordyline australis Grass palm

Although drought adapted, this plant look better with a little irrigation: dry to 4" in spring, 4" to 6" (depending on distance from coast) in summer and fall. No irrigation in winter. Low to moderate nutrient needs. If mulch and compost do not improve appearance, then a light well-balanced supplement in spring will. Removing dead leaves is the only pruning task. If the plant gets too tall, cut the stem to the ground, cut the cane to a better height, and plant the cane in well draining soil in late winter/early spring. The original plant may resprout.

Dianella tasmanica Flax lily

Dry to only 4" in spring and summer, 6" in fall. No irrigation in winter. In the shade it can dry to 6" to 9" spring through fall. Moderate to high nutrient needs; compost, humus and well-balanced organic fertilizers will be required. Deadheading late summer and pulling dead leaves are the only pruning tasks. Easy to propagate from divisions.

Dietes spp. Fortnight lily, African iris

Dry to 1' in spring, 6" in summer, 1' in fall. No irrigation in winter. Moderate nutrient needs and compost and organic supplements will suffice, although an organic supplement may spur more blooms. Deadheading is the only task you need to schedule. Divide if plant becomes too crowded.

Epilobium (Zauschneria) canum California fuchsia or Zauschneria

Southern California native found in coastal-influenced areas. Very drought-adapted and should dry to 6" in spring and summer, 1' the rest of the year. Low nutrient needs and wood chips or mulch is all that is needed. Can reseed, so delay deadheading until late fall. If looking rangy, cut two-thirds in late winter. Start cuttings and plant in late fall/winter.

Eriogonum spp. Buckwheat

Many Southern California natives. Tough and durable. Along the coast they rarely need irrigation once established. Dry to 6" inland in spring and summer, and no irrigation in fall and winter. Can rot in dense and moist soils. Low nutrient needs; nothing more than wood chips or mulch is necessary. Pinch and shear when young to promote bushiness and shape in winter. Seed and plant in late fall/winter. The plants are often short-lived in urban areas.

Euphorbia characias, E. rigida Mediterranean and Gopher spurge

Winter dormant and tough. Dry to 6" spring and summer, 1' in fall and winter. Low nutrient needs; mulch or compost is sufficient. Deadhead late summer. Propagate from cuttings (easy) in early spring. Plant in late winter/spring. It easily reseeds if allowed.

Gaura lindheimeri Gaura

Along coast dry to 6" in spring through fall. No irrigation in winter. Inland dry to 4" year-round. Deadhead after seeds have matured in fall; if reseeding is undesirable, deadhead in summer. Low nutrient needs; nothing but wood chips or mulch is needed. If looking rangy or tired, cut stems nearly to ground late fall/early winter. Plant in winter and spring.

Hemerocallis hybrids Day lily

Dry to 4" in spring, 6" in summer and fall. No irrigation in winter. Moderate nutrient needs; organic supplements will improve blooms. Deadheading in mid-summer and pulling dead leaves in early spring are the only tasks. If it becomes too crowded, then divide.

Iris douglasiana, I. 'Pacific Coast Iris' Pacific coastal iris
Central and northern California coastal native. Dry to 4" winter, 6" in spring, and 9" in summer and fall. Does not need irrigation in summer or fall if in shade along the coast. Low to moderate nutrient needs; a layer of wood chip or mulch will do. Can rot in dense wet soils. Deadhead late spring. Snip dead leaves from plants late winter. Propagate by division in winter.

Juncus mexicanus Rush, mexican
Southern California native. Grass-like perennial. Used in infiltration basins and wet, compacted areas. Can dry to 6" in summer, but only 2" dry in late fall and spring. Low nutrient needs; mulch and compost is all that is needed. If untidy or rangy, cut or mow nearly to ground in fall. Plant and divide in late winter/early spring if used in infiltration areas. With good drainage and moisture it will spread and need corralling.

Juncus patens Rush, California grey
Southern California native. Grass-like perennial treated as a cool season grass. Dry to 6" in summer and 2" in winter and early spring. Moderate nutrient needs; yearly mulch and compost will do. Divide and clean in fall. Plant in early spring. Voracious spreader in moist sandy conditions and it will need corralling.

Kniphofia spp. Red hot poker, Torch lily
Dry to 6" in spring and fall, 4" in summer. No irrigation in winter. Can rot with too much winter moisture. Moderate nutrient needs and mulch and compost will usually do; although it may bloom better with a complete fertilizer in late winter/early spring. Deadhead in summer. Remove dead leaves early spring.

Limonium perezii Sea lavender
Having escaped to the wilds and naturalized along Southern California's coast, this is one tough plant. Cool season grower. Depending on distance from the coast, dry to 4" to 6" in winter and spring, and 6" to 9" in summer and fall. Suffers in dense soils. Low nutrient needs, but sometimes looks better with an organic supplement boost. Along with mulch or compost, add a general-purpose organic fertilizer every other year. Pull dead leaves early spring. Deadhead late spring through early fall, although waiting until late fall will allow it to sow itself. Easily propagated by division.

Lobelia laxiflora Mexican lobelia

Monsoon-adapted and dry to only 6" during summer, but 9" spring and fall. No irrigation in winter. Low nutrient needs; wood chips and mulch will do. Deadhead in fall. If rangy looking, shear to ¼" late winter. Can propagate from root divisions late winter/early spring. Does better inland.

Lomandra spp. Mat rush

Dry to 6" in spring and summer, and 9" in fall. No irrigation in winter. Low to moderate nutrient needs; a thick layer of wood chips, mulch or compost will suffice. Deadhead in late summer. If looking tired or rangy, cut down to 6". Easily propagated from rhizomes.

Lotus scoparius Deerweed

A cool season grower and a Southern California native to coastal-influenced slopes. Dry to just 6" winter and spring, but to 1' in summer and fall along the coast, and 9" inland. Low nutrient needs; wood chips and mulch will suffice. Suffers in dense wet soils. Remove crossing branches, damaged stems, and rangy growth late winter/early spring. Might be short-lived.

Pelargonium Scented geranium

Tougher than the other common geraniums. Dry to 4" in spring, 6" summer and fall. No irrigation in winter. Low to moderate nutrient needs; typically all that is needed is mulch or compost. Tip or shear new growth late winter to induce bushiness. If looking rangy, cut back to succulent growth every few years. Propagates easily from cuttings, which should be taken and planted in winter. Plant late winter/early spring.

Penstemon centranthifolius, P. eatonii, P. heterophyllus, P. pseudospectabilis, P. spectabilis penstemon: Scarlet bugler, Firecracker, Foothill, Desert, Showy

This description is for the Southwestern native perennials, some of which are from Southern California. Drought-adapted and summer-dormant. Dry to only 5" in winter and spring, to 9" in summer and fall. Low nutrients needs; wood chip and mulch will do. They typically suffer in dense, fertile, moist soils. Deadhead mid-fall, in order to let the plants set seed. Can be short-lived in urban areas. Propagate by stem cuttings or seed when it gets cold, typically in early winter. *P. spectabilis* can be propagated by root division.

Phlomis russeliana Turkish sage

Tough. Dries to 6" in spring, summer and fall along the coast, but only 4" to 5" inland. No irrigation in winter. Low to moderate nutrient needs; wood chips, mulch or compost will suffice. May rot in dense soils, especially along the coast. Deadhead in fall. Prune and remove rangy growth in late winter/spring. Easily propagated by root divisions (it spreads by rhizomes) in fall/winter.

Phormium tenax New Zealand flax

Dry to 6" in spring through fall. No irrigation in winter. Will rot in dense wet soils. Do not irrigate in high humidity. Low to moderate nutrient needs; mulch or compost will do. Deadhead in early fall. Pull dead leaves from plant early spring.

Romneya coulteri, R. trichocalyx Matilija poppy, Hairy matilija poppy

Southern California natives. Summer dormant and tough. Dry to only 6" in winter and spring, 9" in summer, and 1' in fall. It may not need any irrigation along the coast. Low nutrient needs; nothing more than wood chips or mulch is necessary. Favors the coast and sandy, coarse soils and suffers in clay soils. If looking rangy or woody, prune stalks down to base in late fall. Not easy to establish or propagate, but once established it travels.

Salvia chiapensis Chiapas sage

Not as tough as the other Salvias. Dry to only 4" in spring, 6" in summer and fall. No irrigation in winter. Moderate nutrient needs; yearly mulch and compost will be needed, along with an occasional organic supplement. Tough to grow in full sun inland. Deadhead in winter. If rangy or twiggy looking, cut back to a couple inches late winter/early spring. Easy to propagate by stem cuttings in winter.

Salvia leucantha Mexican bush sage

Dry to 4" in spring, 6" in summer and fall. No irrigation in winter. Low to moderate nutrient needs. In dense soils needs nothing more than wood chips or mulch; in coarse or sandy soil may require a low dose of organic fertilizers, such as a mix of blood and bone meal as well. If the soil is able to breathe, then this subshrub grows well. Deadhead throughout the year. If looking rangy or unproductive, cut nearly to the ground in late summer/early fall along the coast; in late winter/early spring inland. Can propagate from root divisions.

Salvia spathacea Hummingbird sage
Dry to 4" late winter, early spring, 6" in summer, 9" in fall. No irrigation early winter. Low to moderate nutrient needs; yearly mulch and compost are sufficient. Prefers dry shade and coarse soils, and suffers in wet, dense soils. Deadhead in summer. Easy to propagate from offsets and stem cuttings in winter.

Senecio ineraria, S. viravira Dusty miller
Tough plant. Dries to 4" in spring, but 6" to 9" in summer and fall (depending on distance from coast). No irrigation in winter. Moderate nutrient needs; yearly mulch or compost will be needed, and occasionally organic supplements as well. Will rot in dense, clay soils. Pinch or shear in spring to induce bushiness. If looking rangy, cut back to succulent growth in late winter/early spring.

Silene californica California Indian pink
Southern California native. Dry to 6" in late winter, early spring, 9" in summer, and 1' in fall and early winter. Low nutrient needs; just mulch and compost will do. Suffers in dense moist soils. Deadhead after the seeds have set, typically late summer.

Solidago californica California goldenrod
Southern California native that favors a wet spring. Dry to 4" in late winter/early spring, 6" in late spring/early summer, and 9" in late summer, early fall. No irrigation in late fall/early winter. Low to moderate nutrient needs; a layer of mulch and compost will do. Delay deadheading until seeds have set, usually in late fall.

Sphaeralcea spp. Globe mallow
Includes many Southern California natives and a true desert perennial. Dry to 6" spring, to 1' in summer and fall. No irrigation in winter. Low nutrient needs; just wood chips and mulch will be necessary. Suffers along the coast and in wet/humid environments. If rangy or twiggy looking, cut stems down to ground in late winter/early spring. Propagate by young stem cuttings and seed in winter through spring.

Tagetes lemmonii Mexican marigold or Copper Canyon daisy
Dry to 6" spring through fall along the coast, to 4" inland. No irrigation in winter. Low to moderate nutrient needs; compost plus a light organic fertilizer every other year will improve blooms. If the plant is looking old or rangy, prune nearly to base early spring, after the last flower, but before new growth.

Thalictrum fendleri Meadow rue

Southern California native found in woodland environments. Does best if it does not dry to more than 4" spring and summer, 6" in fall. No irrigation in winter. Moderate nutrient needs, but thrives when given a lot of leafy mulch. Deadhead in early fall. Propagation is easy by dividing the plant.

Tulbaghia violacea Society garlic

Dry to 6" spring through fall. Low to moderate nutrient needs; mulch and compost are sufficient. Deadhead in summer. Pull out dead leaves in late winter. If overcrowded, divide late fall/early winter.

Typha spp. Cattail

Some Southern California natives. Warm season. Cattails need constant moisture and are used for bioremediation in urban areas. They will either grow in standing water or saturated soils. They prefer acidic fertile environments. Leafy debris and compost may be needed to establish a colony. Some varieties are aggressive and will need corralling and dividing in late winter/early spring. Plant in spring.

Verbena lilacina Cedros Island verbena or Lilac verbena

Dry to 4" in late winter/early spring, 6" in late spring to early fall. No irrigation in late fall/early winter. Low nutrient needs; wood chips or mulch will do. Pinch or lightly shear in spring for compactness and containment. Can be short-lived.

Viguiera spp. Desert sunflower, Goldeneye

Some Southern California natives. Mostly found in the deserts and scrub communities. Some are monsoon-adapted. Dry to 6" spring and summer. No irrigation fall or winter. Will rot with too much irrigation. Low nutrient needs; nothing more than wood chips or mulch is needed. If looking rangy, shear to 3" in late winter.

Xanthorrhoea spp. Grass tree

Dry to 6" in spring, 9" summer and fall. No irrigation in winter. Low nutrient needs; nothing but wood chips or mulch is needed. A slow grower and fertilizer will not help. Pull dead leaves in late winter, early spring.

Plant Names

Low Growing and Rooting Perennials:
Common Names to Botanical

African daisy, Freeway daisy *Osteospermum fruticosum*

Aster, California *Symphyotrichum chilense*

Basket of gold *Aurina saxatile*

Beach aster, Sand aster *Lessingia filaginifolia 'Silver Carpet'*

Blue-eyed grass *Sisyrinchium bellum*

Catnip *Nepeta cataria*

Checkerbloom, Prairie mallow *Sidalcea malviflora*

Chamomile *Chamaemelum nobile*

Clover *Trifolium* spp.

Coral bells or Alum root *Heuchera* spp.

Coyote mint *Monardella villosa*

Creeping thyme *Thyme* spp.

Curry and Licorice plants *Helichryum* spp.

Dwarf plumbago *Ceratostigma plumbaginoides*

Dymondia *Dymondia margaretae*

Gazania *Gazania* hybrids

Geranium, ivy geranium, Martha Washington *Pelargonium* spp.

German chamomile *Matricaria recutita*

Germander sage *Salvia chamaedryoides*

Ground morning glory *Convolvulus mauritanicus, C. sabatius*

Gumplant *Grindelia hirsutula*

Hedge nettle, California *Stachys bullata*

Hooker's evening primrose *Oenothera elata hookeri*

Indian mock strawberry *Duchesnea indica*

Lamb's ears *Stachys byzantina*

Lippia *Phyla nodiflora*

Majorcan, Teucrium or fruity germander *Teucrium cossonii*

Mexican daisy, Santa Barbara daisy *Erigeron karvinskianus*

Nasturtium *Tropaeolum* spp.

Peppermint and spearmint *Mentha x piperita, M. spicata*

Potentilla or cinquefoil *Potentilla* spp.

Purple heart, Moses in the cradle *Tradescantia pallida, P. spathacea*

Rupture wort *Herniaria glabra*

Sea pink, Thrift *Armeria* spp.

Seaside daisy *Erigeron glaucus*

Sinaloa sage *Salvia sinaloensis*

Sonoma sage *Salvia sonomensis*

Speedwell, Turkish speedwell, Creeping speedwell *Veronica liwanensis,*
   V. repens
Sundrops *Calylophus berlandieri, C. hartwegii*
Sweet marjoram, oregano *Origanum majorana, O. vulgare*
Tickseed *Coreopsis auriculata 'Nana'*
Trailing mallow *Malvastrum lateritium*
Wild strawberry, sand strawberry *Fragaria chiloensis, F. californica*
Verbena, moss verbena *Verbena peruviana, V. pulchella gracilior, V.*
   tenuisecta
Yarrow *Achillea* spp.
Yerba buena (Yerba yuena) *Clinopodium (Satureja) douglasii*

Larger Perennials: Common Names to Botanical

Angel's hair *Artemisia schmidtiana*
Breath of heaven *Coleonema* spp.
Buckwheat *Eriogonum* spp.
California fuchsia or zauschneria *Epilobium (Zauschneria) canum*
California goldenrod *Solidago californica*
California Indian pink *Silene californica*
California mugwort *Artemisia douglasiana*
Cattail *Typha* spp.
Day lily *Hemerocallis* hybrids
Deerweed *Lotus scoparius*
Desert sunflower, Goldeneye *Viguiera* spp.
Dusty miller *Senecio ineraria, S. viravira*
Flax lily *Dianella tasmanica*
Flax, New Zealand *Phormium tenax*
Fortnight lily, African iris *Dietes* spp.
Gaura *Gaura lindheimeri*
Geranium, scented *Pelargonium*
Globe mallow *Sphaeralcea* spp.
Grass palm *Cordyline australis*
Grass tree *Xanthorrhoea* spp.
Iris, Pacific coastal *Iris douglasiana,* I. 'Pacific Coast Iris'
Kangaroo paws *Anigozanthos* spp.
Lily of the Nile *Agapanthus africanus, A. orientalis*
Matilija poppy, hairy matilija poppy *Romneya coulteri, trichocalyx*
Mat rush *Lomandra* spp.
Meadow rue *Thalictrum fendleri*
Mediterranean and gopher spurge *Euphorbia characias, E. rigida*
Mexican bush sage *Salvia leucantha*
Mexican grass tree, Desert Spoon *Dasylirion* spp.

Mexican lobelia *Lobelia laxiflora*
Mexican marigold or Copper Canyon daisy *Tagetes lemmonii*
Milkweed *Asclepias* spp.
Penstemon: scarlet bugler, firecracker, foothill, desert, showy *Penstemon centranthifolius, eatonii, heterophyllus, pseudospectabilis, spectabilis*
Red hot poker, Torch Lily *Kniphofia* spp.
Rush, California grey *Juncus patens*
Rush, Mexican *Juncus mexicanus*
Sage, hummingbird *Salvia spathacea*
Sage, Chiapas *Salvia chiapensis*
Sea lavender *Limonium perezii*
Society garlic *Tulbaghia violacea*
Spurge, Mediterranean and gopher *Euphorbia characias, E. rigida*
Turkish sage *Phlomis russeliana*
Verbena, Cedros Island or lilac verbena *Verbena lilacina*

Low Growing and Rooting Perennials: Botanical Names to Common

Achillea spp. Yarrow
Armeria spp. Sea pink, thrift
Aurina saxatile Basket of gold
Calylophus berlandieri, C. hartwegii Sundrops
Ceratostigma plumbaginoides Dwarf plumbago
Chamaemelum nobile Chamomile
Clinopodium (Satureja) douglasii Yerba buena (Yerba yuena)
Convolvulus mauritanicus, C. sabatius Ground morning glory
Coreopsis auriculata 'Nana' Tickseed
Duchesnea indica Indian mock strawberry
Dymondia margaretae Dymondia
Erigeron karvinskianus Mexican daisy, Santa Barbara daisy
Erigeron glaucus Seaside daisy
Fragaria chiloensis, F. californica Wild strawberry, sand strawberry
Gazania hybrids Gazania
Grindelia hirsutula Gumplant
Helichryum spp. Curry and licorice plants
Herniaria glabra Rupture wort
Heuchera spp. Coral bells or alum root
Lessingia filaginifolia 'Silver Carpet' California beach aster, sand aster.
Malvastrum lateritium Trailing mallow
Matricaria recutita German chamomile
Mentha x piperita, M. spicata Peppermint and spearmint
Monardella villosa Coyote mint

Monardella odoratissima Mountain pennyroyal

Nepeta cataria Catnip

Oenothera elata hookeri Hooker's evening primrose

Origanum majorana, O. vulgare Sweet marjoram, oregano

Osteospermum fruticosum African daisy, freeway daisy

Pelargonium spp. Common geranium, ivy geranium, Martha Washington

Phyla nodiflora Lippia

Potentilla spp. Potenilla, cinquefoil

Salvia chamaedryoides Germander sage

Salvia leucantha Mexican bush sage

Salvia sinaloensis Sinaloa sage

Salvia sonomensis Sonoma sage

Sidalcea malviflora Checkerbloom, prairie mallow

Sisyrinchium bellum Blue-eyed grass

Stachys bullata California hedge nettle

Stachys byzantina Lamb's ears

Symphyotrichum chilense California aster

Teucrium cossonii Majorcan, teucrium or fruity germander

Thyme spp. Creeping thyme

Tradescantia pallida, P. spathacea Purple heart, Moses in the cradle

Trifolium spp. Clover

Tropaeolum spp. Nasturtium

Verbena peruviana, V. pulchella gracilior, V. tenuisecta Verbena, moss verbena

Veronica liwanensis, V. repens Turkish speedwell, creeping speedwell

Larger Perennials: Botanical Names to Common

Agapanthus africanus, A. orientalis Lily of the Nile

Anigozanthos spp. Kangaroo paws

Artemisia douglasiana California mugwort

Artemisia schmidtiana Angel's hair

Asclepias spp. Milkweed

Coleonema spp. Breath of heaven

Cordyline australis Grass palm

Dasylirion spp. Mexican grass tree, desert spoon

Dianella tasmanica Flax lily

Dietes spp. Fortnight lily, African iris

Epilobium (Zauschneria) canum California fuchsia or zauschneria

Eriogonum spp. Buckwheat

Euphorbia characias, E. rigida Mediterranean and gopher spurge

Gaura lindheimeri Gaura

Hemerocallis hybrids Day lily
Iris douglasiana, I. 'Pacific Coast Iris' Pacific coastal iris
Juncus mexicanus Rush, Mexican
Juncus patens Rush, California grey
Kniphofia spp. Red hot poker, torch lily
Limonium perezii Sea lavender
Lobelia laxiflora Mexican lobelia
Lomandra spp. Mat rush
Lotus scoparius Deerweed
Pelargonium Scented geranium
Penstemon centranthifolius, eatonii, heterophyllus, pseudospectabilis, spectabilis
    Penstemon: scarlet bugler, firecracker, foothill, desert, showy
Phlomis russeliana Turkish sage
Phormium tenax New Zealand flax
Romneya coulteri, trichocalyx Matilija poppy, hairy matilija poppy
Salvia chiapensis Chiapas sage
Salvia spathacea Hummingbird sage
Senecio ineraria, S. *viravira* Dusty miller
Silene californica California Indian pink
Solidago californica California goldenrod
Sphaeralcea spp. Globe mallow
Tagetes lemmonii Mexican marigold or Copper Canyon daisy
Thalictrum fendleri Meadow rue
Tulbaghia violacea Society garlic
Typha spp. Cattail
Verbena lilacina Cedros Island verbena or lilac verbena
Viguiera spp. Desert sunflower, goldeneye
Xanthorrhoea spp. Grass tree

Shrubs

Shrubs are some of the most California Friendly plants. It is not because they are the most drought tolerant plants—what beats yucca—but because they provide the greatest number of benefits per gallon of water.

The benefits of shrubs include:

1. They use less water and resources than many perennials and most trees.

2. They have long lives and require less overall maintenance.

3. They tolerate urban soil better than smaller plants.

4. They are intimately connected to biological processes because the majority are animal-pollinated or have their seeds distributed by animals. This also means they produce less allergens.

5. And, for the gardener, they forgive and recover gracefully from accidents, mistakes, and mishaps.

Technically, a shrub is a plant not growing to more than 25' with many woody stems originating from its base. This chapter provides general growing tips and then specific recommendations for both the low-growing, ground-hugging shrubs and the larger ones.

California wild rose, lavender, manzanita, toyon and Pacific wax myrtle grace this beautiful landscape. Energy Resource Center, Downey.

General Growing Tips

Below are general guidelines for growing shrubs and includes information on soils, irrigation, fertilization, pruning and renewal. Following this section are specific recommendations for individual shrubs.

Soil

The shrubs listed in this chapter grow naturally in biologically rich areas, such as chaparral, streamside, and woodland environments. The soils in these environments are rich, too, teeming with bacterial and fungal life. While these shrubs can grow in almost any type of soil, they favor several key characteristics;

- The soil should contain medium amounts of organic matter and be mulched as well. Amendments should include thick and carbonous organics such as wood chips as well as quick to decompose ones such as compost. Too much carbon is better than too much compost. Desert shrubs are an exception; they prefer soils low in organic material.

- The soil's pH should be neutral to slightly acidic—from 6 to 7 pH. Most urban soils are already in this range. However, desert, scrub and some chaparral shrubs favor slightly alkaline soils.

- Good drainage is essential. Good drainage supports plant health by reducing the chances of toxicity, ensuring the movement of gases, and encouraging healthy microbes.

Irrigation / Water Requirements

All the shrubs included in this chapter are tough. The soils around most shrubs can dry to 6" or more, some even to 1'. This means that the irrigation needs to run a long time to get the water deep, and then be off for a long time until waiting while the soil dries. As an example, a large shrub in clay soil that dries to 1' will require about 150 gallons of water, but it may take that soil about 3 weeks to dry to 1'. For a more thorough explanation, please refer to the Irrigation chapters.

Many of the plants included in this chapter are summer-dormant and the irrigation recommendations honor that. Stimulating a plant during its dormancy may shorten its life and encourage pest problems.

Coyote brush goes dormant late summer. Reducing irrigation favors this natural cycle and can extend the life of tough summer dormant plants such as these.

Fertilizing / Fertilization

Most of the shrubs in this chapter come from biologically rich areas with biologically complex soils. Most of these shrubs favor semi-fertile soils with both bacterial and fungal life. Wood chips, mulch, and compost are usually enough. Fertilizers might be needed in coarse and sandy soils; a general-purpose organic fertilizer in spring is sufficient. Activated sludge or animal meals mixed with the woody mulch is an ideal supplement.

Note that desert, scrub and some chaparral plants favor soils much lower in organic matter. Gravel, decomposed granite (dg) and river rock are common mulches for these shrubs. Fertilizers are not recommended, even organic ones. Fertilizers can shorten these plants' lives and encourage pest problems.

Dense and woody mulch is preferred around plants with low nutrient needs. The mulch pictured above protects the soil, conserves water, suppresses weeds, and provides low levels of nutrients to the sagebrush and trailing sage after it has decomposed.

Pruning

Only topiary shrubs need constant pruning. The shrubs below will benefit from strategic pruning, but not constant. The most frequent pruning tasks are lightly shearing for compactness and containment, and thinning to remove unhealthy stems, improve aesthetic structure, and increase air flow. Any shrub that needs regular pruning, particularly shearing, should be removed and replanted with something more suitable.

Unlike the larger shrubs, low-growing, rooting shrubs can be maintained with a variety of pruning approaches: mowing, pinching, shearing, thinning and weed whacking. But, as with the larger shrubs, pruning should be strategic and limited.

As a Rule

■ Never remove more than one-third of a plant; one-fifth is usually better.

■ Avoid pruning out of season because it increases chances of climatic injury and pest infestations.

■ Never prune when the soil is wet—soil compaction is inevitable and creates a slew of problems. Work when the soil is dry or only slightly moist.

The island mallow (*Malva assurgentiflora*) pictured has been properly pruned. The interior has been cleaned of crossing and weak stems, the larger branches have been cut back to live nodes, and selective pinching will help keep it compact. Arlington Garden, Pasadena.

Renewal: When is the Best Time?

An old or unhealthy plant increases risk in a landscape. These vulnerable plants are more prone to breakage; they require more resources and pesticides to sustain; and they may help spread diseases and pests—all of which increases economic costs. A smart gardener will remove a plant before it becomes a liability. The characteristics of a plant that needs replacing include:

- Older leaves and limbs are dead. On trees, 50% or more of the trunk has either dead limbs or no limbs

- The living foliage is only at the very end of the branches, instead of throughout the entire branch.

- During summer the plant drops more leaves than usual.

- When a bud or disease infestation is difficult to control, if possible at all.

- A plant does not recover, or is slow to recover from injury.

- A plant shows signs of decay, such as mushrooms coming up from its base and roots, or shelf fungi along its trunk.

The *Encelia*, buckwheat and sagebrush pictured at left are generally short-lived plants and no amount of pruning will bring them back. These plants should be removed.

Individual Plant Care

The plants below are listed by their botanic names. They are also cross-referenced by their common names at the end of the chapter.

Note: *Irrigation requirements are expressed in the amount of inches a soil should dry before receiving supplemental water. Of course, if a soil never dries to prescribed depth, which is not uncommon, then the plant requires no irrigation.* ■

Low, Rooting and Spreading

Acacia redolens, A. r. 'Desert Carpet' Desert carpet
Dry to 6" year round. Low nutrient needs; nothing more than mulch is needed. However, because this plant is usually planted on slopes, a mild, well-balanced organic supplement should be applied every 2 or 3 years will help improve appearance and increase blooms. Too much moisture and fertilizer will shorten its life. Push stems into soil to root in late winter/early spring. Thrips and mites can be problems.

Acalypha californica California copperleaf
Tough Southern California native. After established, dry to 4"–6" in winter/spring, and 9" to 1' in fall. No irrigation in summer. Low nutrient needs; gravel and stone are the best mulches; nothing richer than wood chips is ever needed. Suffers greatly in dense soils. Pinch or lightly shear in winter for compactness. Thin and remove rangy stems, crossing branches, and damaged wood in late fall/winter.

Adenostoma fasciculatum 'Prostrate' Prostrate chamise
Southern California native. Dries to 6" late winter/early spring and to 1' late spring through late summer. No irrigation the rest of the year. Low nutrient needs; nothing more than a light layer of wood chips or mulch is needed. Too much moisture and fertilizers will either shorten its life or cause it to rot. Suffers in full sun inland. Push stems into the soil to root in winter.

Arctostaphylos spp. 'Prostrate' Trailing manzanita
Some Southern California natives. Prefers a moist winter and spring, drying to only 4", and some moisture the rest of the year, drying to 6" summer and fall. Moderate nutrient needs and mulch; compost or humus may be needed yearly. Will suffer in full sun inland. Push stems into ground to root in late in fall/winter.

Artemisia caucasica Silver spreader

Dry to 6" in spring, 9" to 1' summer and fall (depending on distance from coast). No irrigation in winter. Low nutrient needs; wood chips and mulch will do. It will rot in dense, wet soils. If rangy or too woody, then cut back to succulent wood late winter/early spring. Push stems into soil to root in late fall/winter.

Artemisia 'Powis Castle' Silver sage

Dry to 6" in spring and fall, 4" in summer. No irrigation in winter. Low nutrient needs; wood chips and mulch will do. Favors good drainage. Pinch or lightly shear to create bushiness. Although it does not require a lot of pruning, remove rangy stems in early spring to improve appearance. Might be short-lived.

Baccharis pilularis Coyote brush

Southern California native. Dry to 6" in spring, 9" to 1' summer and fall (depending on distance from coast). No irrigation in winter. Low nutrient needs; wood chips, mulch and compost will suffice. Too much moisture and fertilizer will shorten its life. Pinch and shear in early spring to induce bushiness. Push stems into soil to root in late fall/winter.

Berberis (Mahonia) aquifolium, B. fremontii, B. pinnata, B. repens Oregon grape, Desert mahonia, California holly grape, Creeping mahonia

Many but not all are California natives. Dry to 4" in spring, 6" in summer and fall. No irrigation in winter. Moderate nutrient needs but prefers acidic soils. Mulch, compost and an organic supplement will be needed every 2 to 3 years. Will sunburn if in full sun inland. Shear to contain and remove twiggy growth any time of year. If looking rangy or tired, cut nearly to the ground in late winter/early spring. Spreads by stolons and propagating from root division is easy in spring.

Carissa macrocarpa 'Green Carpet' Prostrate natal plum

Dry to 4" in spring, 6" in summer and fall. No irrigation in winter. Moderate nutrient needs; yearly mulch and compost may have to be supplemented occasionally with a well-balanced organic fertilizer. Pinch and lightly shear to induce bushiness in early spring. Push stems into soil to root in late winter/early spring.

Ceanothus gloriosus, C. griseus horizontalis, C. maritimus California lilac
Some California natives. Dry to 6" in spring and summer, to 1'
in fall. No irrigation in winter. Low to moderate nutrient needs;
mulch and compost may be needed yearly. Too much moisture and
nutrients can shorten an already short life. Suffers in too much sun
inland. Pinch or lightly shear in late fall to increase bushiness. Push
stems into soil to root in winter.

Coprosma repens Creeping mirror plant
Dry to 4" spring and summer, 6" fall and winter. Moderate nutri-
ent needs and mulch, compost and humus are all that is required.
Do not irrigate when excessively humid as *Coprosma* is prone to rot.
Push stems into soil to root in late winter/early spring.

Cotoneaster dammeri 'Lowfast' Bearberry cotoneaster
Dry to 4" in spring, 6" summer and fall. No irrigation in winter.
Low to moderate nutrient needs; typically mulch and compost are
all that is needed. Cotoneaster does not respond well to heavy pruning, so only lightly shear to induce bushiness in early spring. Push
stems into the soil to root in winter.

Hypericum calycinum Creeping St. Johnswort
Dry to 4" in spring, 6" in summer and fall. No irrigation in winter.
Low nutrient needs; wood chips and mulch are sufficient. If looking
rangy or twiggy, mow or shear to 3" in winter. Spreads by rhizomes
and easily propagated by root divisions in spring.

Iva hayesiana Poverty weed or San Diego marsh-elder
Southern California native that only requires irrigation in the spring,
drying to 6". No irrigation the rest of the year. Low nutrient needs;
wood chips are sufficient. Suffer in acidic and moist soils. If it gets
rangy, mow or shear in late fall. Push stems into soil to root in late
fall/winter.

Juniperus spp. Creeping / prostrate junipers
Along the coast dry to 9" in spring and summer, to 1' in fall. No
irrigation in winter. In the hotter and drier (inland) areas dry to 4"
in spring, 6" summer and fall. No irrigation in winter. These plants
are easily overwatered in dense, clay soils. Low nutrient needs;
mulch and compost will do. Junipers need little pruning, but pinch
and shear to induce bushiness in late winter. Wash foliage occasionally to remove dust and mites. Push stems into the soil to root in
winter/early spring.

Lantana montevidensis Purple trailing lantana

Dry to 4" in spring, 6" in summer and fall. No irrigation in winter. Requires almost no irrigation in the shade. Low nutrient needs; wood chips, mulch and compost will be enough. Suffers from too much moisture and fertilization. If looking rangy or twiggy, mow or shear to 3" in late winter/early spring. Push stems into the soil to root in winter.

Myoporum 'Pacificum', M. parvifolium Pacific myoporum, Creeping myoporum

Tough plant, especially along the coast, where it can dry to 6" in spring, 9" in summer and fall. In the hotter, drier areas, dry to only 4" in spring and 6" summer and fall. No irrigation in winter. It will rot in dense, wet soils. Low nutrient needs; mulch and compost will suffice. Too much water and nutrients will shorten its life. Pinch or lightly shear in late winter/early spring to induce bushiness. Push stems into the ground to root in winter. *Myoporum* are susceptible to thrips.

Phlomis italica Balearic Island sage

Tough plant. Dries to 6" in spring, summer and fall along the coast, but only 4" to 5" inland. No irrigation in winter. Low to moderate nutrient needs; wood chips, mulch and compost will suffice. May rot in dense soils, especially along the coast. Needs shade in the desert. Deadhead in fall. Prune and remove rangy growth in late winter/spring. Easily propagated by root divisions (it spreads by suckers) in fall/winter.

Rhaphiolepis indica 'Ballerina' Indian hawthorn

Dries to 6" year round. Low to moderate nutrient needs; mulch, compost and humus are adequate, but an occasional well-balanced organic supplement will improve flowering. Pinch or lightly shear in spring to induce bushiness. Thin to improve structural appearance in late winter/early spring. Push stems into soil to root in winter. Prone to mites in dusty, dry locations; occasionally wash foliage.

Rosmarinus officinalis Rosemary, all types

Dry to 4" in spring, 6" to 9' in summer and fall (depending on distance from coast). No irrigation in winter. Moderate nutrient needs; if mulch or compost cannot be given yearly because of its dense nature, then well-balanced organic supplements will be needed every other year. Be careful—too much water and fertilizer will shorten its useful life. Pinch or lightly shear throughout the year to induce bushiness. Never prune more than ⅓ of the plant per year. Push stems into the ground to root in winter. Prone to mealybugs, mites and thrips in dusty and dry locations; washing foliage twice a year helps.

Symphoricarpos albus, S. mollis Creeping snowberry

Southern California woodland plants. Dry to 5" in spring, fall and winter. No irrigation in summer. Low to moderate nutrient needs; wood chips, mulch and compost is all that is needed. Suffers in dense soils. Pinch or lightly shear in spring to induce bushiness. Remove rangy, twiggy growth any time of year. Spreads by rhizomes and propagation from root division is easy in late winter/early spring.

Larger Shrubs

Abutilon palmeri Indian mallow

Southern California native. Once established, dry to 6" in spring, 1' in summer. No irrigation in fall and winter. Low nutrient needs; a light layer of wood chips and gravel will suffice. Does not respond well to pruning. Pinch and lightly shear in spring to encourage bushiness. Remove sickly, rangy stems late winter/early spring.

Acca sellowiana (Feijoa sellowiana) Pineapple guava

Dry to 9" in spring and summer, 6" in fall when it is setting fruit. No irrigation in winter. Moderate nutrient needs; for best fruit and flower a complete organic fertilizer will be needed yearly. Prune sickly and damaged branches in late fall/early spring.

Alyogyne huegelii Blue hibiscus

A cool season plant that prefers only drying to 6" in winter and spring, but 9" in summer and fall. Low nutrient needs, but yearly mulch or compost will increase flowering. Can rot in dense, wet soils. Pinch or lightly shear for bushiness any time of year. Thin and cut back in winter.

Anisodontea xhypomandarum Cape mallow

Dry to 6" spring through fall. No irrigation in winter. Low nutrient needs; maintaining a light layer of wood chips or mulch works well. Suffers in poor draining soils. Too much water and nutrients will shorten its aesthetic life as it gets woody fast. Pinch or lightly shear to promote bushiness in spring.

***Arctostaphylos* spp.** Manzanita

Some Southern California natives from the mountains. Prefers a moist winter and spring, drying to just 4", but to 6" in summer, and to 1' in fall. Moderate nutrient needs; mulch, or compost may be needed yearly. It tolerates typical garden conditions. Will suffer in full sun inland.

***Artemisia* spp.** Wormwood and Sagebrush

Many Southern California natives. Dry to 6" in spring, 9" to 1' summer and fall (depending on distance from coast). No irrigation in winter. Low nutrient needs; wood chips and mulch will do. It will rot in poor draining or wet soils. If rangy or too woody, cut back to succulent wood late winter/early spring. Artemisia ages faster in typical garden conditions than in the wild.

Baccharis* spp.** See ***Baccharis pilularis in the Woody, Rooting, Spreading Shrubs section above.

***Buddleja* spp.** Butterfly bush

Winter dormant. Dries to 4" or 6" spring/early summer (depending on distance from coast.), 6" to 9" late summer and fall. No irrigation in winter. Low to moderate nutrient needs; yearly mulch with an occasional organic supplement will help keep the plant showy. Favors coarse soils and suffers with compaction. Pinch or lightly shear to promote bushiness in spring. Cut older, rangy stems to ground in winter. Do not remove suckers as they will become the new plant.

Caesalpinia pulcherrima Mexican poininciana or Red bird of paradise

Dries to 6" spring, and 6" to 9" summer and fall (depending on distance from coast). Low nutrient needs; mulch and compost will do. Favors well-draining soils and suffers without air round its roots. Pinch or lightly shear to promote bushiness in spring. Cut the stems that are dead, dying or damaged to the ground in winter.

Calliandra californica, C. eriophylla Baja fairy duster and Fairy duster
Found naturally in the washes and plains of Baja California and
Southern California. Dry to only 4" to 6" late winter/spring, 9" to
1' summer and early fall. No irrigation in late fall/early winter. Low
nutrient needs; wood chips and a light layer of gravel are sufficient.
Will suffer in dense soils. Pinch or lightly shear to promote bushiness in early spring. Remove rangy, damaged and poorly structured
branches in winter.

Carissa* spp.** Natal Plum See ***Carissa macrocarpa in the Woody, Rooting,
Spreading Shrubs section above.

Carpenteria californica Bush anemone
Native to the canyons and crevices of California's foothills. Prefers
drying to only 4" late winter through early spring, to 6" to 8" in
spring through fall. No irrigation in winter. Moderate nutrient
needs; compost, humus and coffee grounds might be needed yearly.
Carpenteria favors acidic soil. Will suffer in dense wet soils. Pinch or
lightly shear in summer to promote bushiness. Does not respond
well to aggressive pruning. Will not survive in full sun inland.

Ceanothus* spp.** See ***Ceanothus in the Woody, Rooting, Spreading Shrubs
section above.

***Cercocarpus* spp.** Mountain mahogany
Many native to Southern California's foothills and mountains. Tough
plant. Dry to 6" spring, 1' summer and fall. No irrigation in winter.
Low nutrient needs; wood chips and mulch is the only requirement.
If along the coast, thin in late spring to increase air circulation and
warmth; if inland, light shear in early spring to induce bushiness
and root shading.

***Cistus* spp.** Rockrose
A cool season grower and durable. Inland it dries to 6" in late win-
ter/early spring, 9" in late spring/early summer, and to 1' in late
summer/early fall. No irrigation in late fall/ early winter. Along the
coast dry to 1' winter through early summer. No irrigation the rest
of the year. Low nutrient needs; wood chips or mulch every other
year is all that is needed. Too much water and nutrients will hasten
the demise of an already short-lived plant. Pinch or lightly shear to
create compactness in late winter/early spring. Rockrose suffers with
pruning and if it needs a lot, then replace the plant.

Cassia artemisiodes See ***Senna***

Cercidium spp. Palo Verde

Several species native to Southern California's desert. Monsoon-adapted and dries to 1' in winter, no irrigation in spring, 1' in summer, no irrigation in fall. Do not irrigate in high humidity as Cercidium is prone to mildew. Low nutrient needs; a light layer of wood chips is adequate. Can be pinched or lightly sheared any time of year. Prune rangy, crossing and damaged branches and stems late winter/early spring.

Coprosma spp. See **Coprosma** in the Woody, Rooting, Spreading Shrubs section above.

Correa spp. Australian fuchsia

Dry to about 6" year round along the coast, but only 4" inland. Moderate nutrient needs; in addition to compost, an occasional well-balanced organic fertilizer may be needed to spur blooms. Pinch or lightly shear for compactness. Thin rangy growth late winter/early spring.

Cotoneaster spp. Cotoneaster See **Cotoneaster** in the Woody, Rooting, Spreading Shrubs section above.

Dalea spp. Indigo bush

A desert native with a few from Southern California. Dry to 1' in spring and summer. No irrigation the rest of the year. Low nutrient needs; only wood chips and gravel are necessary. Too much water and/or nutrients will greatly shorten its life. Will suffer in dense soils and along the coast. Pinch and remove rangy stems late winter. It does not respond well to a hard pruning.

Dasylirion spp. Mexican grass tree or Desert spoon

Tough, but monsoon-adapted and performs better if it only dries to 6" during summer, to 6" to 9" in spring and fall. No irrigation in winter. Low nutrient needs; wood chips and mulch will suffice. Plant late winter/early spring.

Dendromecon harfordii, D. rigida Island bush poppy and Bush poppy

Southern California natives. Cool season growers. Dries to 1' in late fall/spring. No irrigation the rest of the year. Low nutrient needs; maintaining a light layer of wood chips and gravel will suffice. Suffers from summer irrigation if in dense soil. Pinch or lightly shear for compactness winter through early summer. If rangy, twiggy, or lopsided, cut back by half in late fall.

***Dodonaea* spp.** Hopseed

Dry to 5"–7" year round, depending on distance from coast. Low nutrient needs; mulch and compost will suffice. Good drainage ensures a long life. Pinch or lightly shear for compactness in winter/spring. Thin rangy stems and branches late fall/early winter.

Encelia californica Bush sunflower or California encelia

Southern California coastal native and a cool-season grower. Dry to 6" late winter through early spring; to 1' late spring through early fall. No irrigation late fall/early winter. Will suffer in wet soils. Low nutrient needs; a thin layer of wood chips will do. Deadhead in early fall. Lightly shear for containment in spring. If rangy looking, cut by three-quarters in winter. Can be short lived.

***Eriogonum* spp.** Buckwheat

Some California natives. Cool season growers. Dries to 1' winter/spring along the coast. No irrigation summer through fall. Inland dries to 1' year-round. Low nutrient needs; maintaining a light layer of wood chips and gravel will suffice. Will suffer in dense soils and summer irrigation. Deadhead after flowers have set seed if regeneration is desired. Does not respond well to pruning; only pinch or lightly shear for compactness winter through early summer. Often short-lived in urban environments.

Fallugia paradoxa Apache plume

Southern California native to deserts. Monsoon-adapted. Tolerates no irrigation in spring, fall or winter, but dry to only 6" in summer inland. No irrigation along coast. Low nutrient needs; wood chips or mulch or a fine layer of gravel will do. Suffers in dense soils. Start stem cuttings winter. Plant early in late winter/early spring.

***Fremontodendron* spp.** Fremontia or Flannel bush

Southern California natives found along washes. Dry to 1' in late fall and winter. No irrigation the rest of the year. Low nutrient needs; wood chips and mulch are sufficient. Suffer in dense soils and summer irrigation. Pinch and lightly shear for structure winter through early spring. Thin and remove rangy branches late fall/early winter. Caution: always wear eye protection, long-sleeved shirt and gloves to protect against its leaf hairs, an obnoxious irritant.

Gambelia* (*Galvezia*) *speciosa Island bush snapdragon

Native to Southern California's islands. Dries to 1' year round. Low nutrient needs; a layer of mulch will suffice. Prefers coarse soils. Pinch or slightly prune for compactness between winter and spring. Thin rangy stems and prune to contain size in late fall/winter.

Grevillea spp. Grevillea

Dry to 6" in winter/spring, 9" to 1' in summer/fall, depending on distance from coast and amount of sun. Low nutrient needs; a layer of mulch or compost will do. Note: avoid fertilizers with high amounts of phosphorus; Grevillea is phosphorus-intolerant. Pinch and lightly shear for compactness in spring. Remove rangy stems and cut back unwanted growth in late winter/early spring.

Hamelia patens Firebush or Texas firecracker bush

A tough tropical. Dries to 6" year round. Moderate nutrient needs; mulch and compost will be needed and, occasionally, a well-balanced organic fertilizer in late winter. Pinch to induce bushiness in spring. Remove rangy stems and control size in late winter/early spring.

Heteromeles arbutifolia Toyon

Southern California native found along the coast, in chaparral communities, and in the Sierra foothills. Dry to 1' year round along the coast, only to 9" inland. Low nutrient needs; wood chips or mulch are adequate. Suffers from a variety of problems in areas of poor air circulation. Pinch or slightly shear winter/spring. Thin rangy stems and prune to improve structure late fall/early winter.

Hyptis emoryi Desert lavender

Desert native from the washes of eastern Southern California. Dry to 1' in winter through spring. No irrigation the rest of the year. Low nutrient needs; only a thin layer of wood chips is needed. Too much moisture or fertilizer will shorten its life. Desert lavender suffers greatly in dense soils. Does not respond well to pruning; only pinch or lightly shear in late winter/early spring.

Isomeris arborea Bladderpod or California cleome

Dries to 1' in winter/spring. No irrigation the rest of the year. Too much winter moisture will kill it. Low nutrient needs; a layer of wood chips is sufficient. Becomes woody and short-lived with too much water and nutrients. Pinch or lightly shear late winter/early spring to promote bushiness. Bladderbod does not like pruning, but you can clean a twiggy and dead interior at anytime. Do not deadhead until seeds have matured in fall.

Justicia californica, J. spicigera Chuparosa and Mexican honeysuckle.

J. *californica*. is native to the interior washes of Southern California. Both dry to 1' year round. No irrigation in summer and fall along the coast. Low nutrient needs; wood chips, mulch and compost will do. Suffers in dense soils. Pinch for compactness and thin for structure in late winter.

***Keckiella* spp.** Heart leaved penstemon, Chaparral beardtongue, Climbing penstemon

> Some Southern California coastal natives. Dry to 1' year round along the coast, but inland dry to 1' in winter/spring, to 9" in summer/fall. No irrigation in the shade, either along the coast or inland. Low nutrient needs; just a layer of mulch or compost is needed. Pinch or lightly shear for compactness in spring. Thin rangy, weak and structurally poor stems late winter/early spring.

***Lantana* spp.** Lantana

> Dry to 6" in spring, 6" to 9" in summer and early fall. No irrigation in late fall and winter. Low to moderate nutrient needs; besides a layer of compost, a light organic fertilizer higher in phosphorus (such as bone meal) will be needed. Pinch or lightly shear for compactness in spring. Repetitive shearing will lead to a woody, unsightly interior. Thin plant and remove rangy growth in late winter/early spring. Never remove more than one-fifth of the plant at a time.

Larrea tridentata Creosote bush

> Southern California native found throughout the warm eastern interior. Dry to 6" in late winter/early spring and to 1' in late spring/early winter. It might not need the irrigation, but often looks better with just a little. Low nutrient needs; wood chips, mulch or compost will do. Pinch or lightly shear for bushiness in spring. Remove rangy stems and crossing interior branches in late winter/early spring.

***Lavandula* spp.** Lavender

> Dry to 4" in spring, 6" in summer and fall. No irrigation in winter. Avoid irrigation in periods of high humidity. Low to moderate nutrient needs; typically nothing more than mulch and compost are needed. Plants in coarse soils may need a light organic supplement. Pinch for compactness, but only infrequently, in spring. If looking rangy, prune stems nearly to base in late winter/early spring. Lavender usually loses its aesthetic charm after 3 to 5 years; plan on periodic replacement.

Leonotis leonurus Lion's tail

> Dry to 4" in spring, 6" to 8" in summer and fall. No irrigation in winter. Low to moderate nutrient needs; just a layer of mulch or compost is necessary. Pinch or lightly shear for bushiness in spring. If rangy looking, cut back to lowest live node—more than half the plant—in late winter/early spring. Plan on replacing the plant every 4 to 6 years.

Leucadendron Cultivars, L. discolor, L. tinctum Leucadendron

Dry to 9" along the coast and 6" inland year round. Low to moderate nutrient needs; usually compost and mulch is sufficient. Does not tolerate fertilizers with a lot of phosphorus; like Grevillea it is phosphorus-intolerant. Acidic organics, such as coffee grounds, are preferred. Pinch for compactness and thin rangy, crossing stems in spring.

Leucophyllum spp. Texas ranger

Monsoon-adapted. Prefers drying to 6" in spring, 9" in summer. No irrigation the rest of the year. Low nutrient needs; wood chips, mulch and compost will do. Suffers in dense and/or acidic soils. Pinch or lightly shear in spring to promote bushiness. The plant's branches, stems and leaves shade its roots and it dislikes heavy pruning (pruning exposes the soil to the sun), but, if it is needed, prune in late winter/early spring only.

Malva (Lavatera) assurgentiflora, M. maritima Island mallow and
Tree mallow

Southern California coastal native. Dry to 1' in spring through fall along the coast, 6" to 9" inland. No irrigation in winter. Low to moderate nutrient needs; a 2" layer of mulch or compost will do. If in sandy or coarse soils, it will perform better when given a diluted well-balanced organic fertilizer in spring. Pinch and lightly shear to contain in spring. Remove crossing, damaged and rangy stems late winter/early spring.

Mimulus aurantiacus Sticky monkey flower

Southern California native found in the coastal-influenced areas and a cool season grower. Dry to 9" in fall and winter, and 1' spring and summer. Low nutrient needs; only wood chips, mulch or compost is needed. Too much water, fertilizer or pruning will shorten an already short life. Pinch regularly to encourage dense branching. Deadhead in late spring to encourage another bloom cycle. Thin twiggy growth to active nodes in late fall. Plan on frequent replacement.

Morella (Myrica) californica Pacific wax myrtle

Coastal California native and a cool season grower. Can dry to 1' along the coast year round, but only 6" where it is hot and dry. Low to moderate nutrient needs; as well as with mulch and compost, an organic well-balanced fertilizer may be needed every other year. Responds well to pinching and shearing in every season but summer. Remove rangy and rubbing stems in late fall/early winter.

Myoporum spp. Myoporum See **Myoporum** in the Woody, Rooting, Spreading Shrubs section above.

Parkinsonia spp. Palo Verde See **Cercidium spp.** above.

Perovskia spp. Russian sage
> Dry to 6" in spring, 9" summer and fall. No irrigation in winter. Low nutrient needs; wood chips and mulch will do. Suffers in dense soils. Deadhead in late summer. Cut to lowest active node, nearly to ground, in late winter/early spring. Can be propagated by cuttings in winter through spring

Phlomis fruticosa Jerusalem sage
> Dry to 6" in spring, summer and fall along the coast, but only 4" to 5" inland. No irrigation in winter. Low to moderate nutrient needs; wood chips, mulch and compost will suffice. May rot in dense soils, more so along the coast. Prefers a little shade inland. Deadhead in fall. If looking rangy or tired, cut stems to lowest active node in late winter/ early spring.

Plumbago auriculata Cape plumbago
> Dry to 6" in spring through early fall inland; along the coast, dry to 6" in spring and to 1' in summer and fall. No irrigation in winter. Low nutrient needs; a light layer of wood chips or mulch will do. Pinch or shear anytime to contain and shape. If looking rangy, twiggy or unsightly, prune down by two-thirds in late winter/early spring.

Prosopis spp. Mesquite
> Desert native with an extensive root system. Dries to 9" or 1' throughout the year. Its size is related to amount of moisture it receives. May not need any irrigation along the coast. Low nutrient needs; a light layer of wood chips and gravel is sufficient. Pinch or shear to contain in spring. Remove dead, damaged or rangy branches and stems in late winter/early spring.

Prunus ilicifolia, P. i. lyonii Hollyleaf cherry, Catalina cherry
> Southern California coastal and island natives. Dry to 6" winter through early spring, between 6" and 9" in late spring through summer (depending on distance from coast). No irrigation in winter. Low to moderate nutrient needs; wood chips and mulch is usually enough, but organic supplements are needed as well in coarse soils. P. lyonii is much more tolerant of clay soils and moisture. Pinch or shear for compactness and containment in winter through spring. Remove crossing interior and rangy growth in late fall/early winter.

Quercus spp. scrub oaks
Many Southern California natives. Dry to 6" in spring and to 1' the rest of the year. No irrigation may be needed along the coast. Low nutrient needs; wood chips and gravel will do. Pinch or shear whenever needed. Prune August through September after all growth has stopped.

Rhamnus (Frangula) californica, R. crocea Coffeeberry, Redberry
Southern California native found in canyons and coastal slopes. Dry to 6" in late winter/early spring, to 1' late spring/summer. No irrigation in fall. The greater the shade, the less irrigation needed. Low nutrient needs; a layer of mulch or compost is adequate. Pinch or lightly shear for compactness in spring. Coffeeberry's canopy shades its roots and the plant does not respond well to pruning; only remove the rangy and damaged growth in late winter.

Rhus spp. Lemonade berry, Pink flowering sumac, Sugar bush
Southern California natives. Dry to just 6" in winter, 9" in spring and, if along the coast, give no irrigation the rest of the year; if inland, dry to 1' summer and fall. Low nutrient needs; nothing more than wood chips or mulch is necessary. Pinch or shear for compactness and containment. Prune to improve structure and air flow in late fall/early winter.

Ribes spp. Gooseberry and Currant
Many Southern California natives. If in shade, dry to 9" winter and spring, and give no irrigation the rest of the year. If in full sun, dry to 6" winter and spring, and 9" summer and fall. Low to moderate nutrient needs; while mulch and compost are usually enough, a well-balanced organic supplement every other year will improve the plant's appearance, especially in quick draining soils. Pinch or shear to induce bushiness anytime. If looking rangy or tired, cut all stems back to lowest active node in late fall/early winter.

Rosa californica California wild rose
Southern California native found in and along canyons and creeks. Dry to 6" spring and summer, and to 1' fall and winter. Moderate nutrient needs; along with a layer of mulch or compost, an organic well-balanced supplement will be needed occasionally. Deadhead throughout the year for repeat blooms. Thin, cut back and remove rangy growth in late fall/early winter. Like most roses, R. *californica* is prone to aphids, mildew, mites and thrips.

Rosmarinus officinalis: See **Rosmarinus** in the Woody, Rooting, Spreading Shrubs section above.

Russelia equisetiformis Coral fountain

Dry to only 6" along the coast every season but winter, only to 4" inland. No irrigation in winter for either location. Moderate nutrient needs; along with mulch or compost, a well-balanced organic supplement will be needed, particularly in coarse soils. Cut rangy stems back to base anytime. If looking tired or unsightly, cut entire plant back to its base in late winter/early spring.

Salvia, also see **Salvia** in the chapter Perennials.

Salvia 'Allen Chickering', S. apiana, S. Bee's Bliss, S. brandegei, S. canariensis, S. clevelandii, S. 'Dara's Choice', S. greggii, S. leucophylla, S. mellifera, S. microphylla Allen Chickering sage, White sage, Bee's bliss, Santa Rosa Island sage, Canary Island sage, Cleveland Sage, Autumn sage, Purple sage, Black sage, Cherry sage, Mrs. Beard sage

These are the most drought-tolerant sages of this large genus and most are native to the coastal-influenced areas of Southern California. Dry to 6" winter and spring and to 1' summer and fall. Low nutrient needs; wood chips or mulch will suffice. Too much water and nutrients will shorten an already short life. If looking rangy or tired, cut back to lowest active node in late fall/early winter. Suffers with too much pruning and never cut into older wood. For regeneration, do not deadhead until after the plant has set seed.

Santolina chamaecyparissus Lavender cotton

Along the coast dry to 6" in late winter and spring, and to 1' the rest of the year. Inland, dry to 6" in late winter/early spring, and 6" to 9" the rest of the year (depending on amount of sun). Low nutrient needs; a layer of mulch or compost is sufficient. Deadhead in summer. Pinch or shear anytime to induce bushiness. If looking rangy, prune to base in late winter.

Senna artemisioides, C. phyllodinea Feathery cassia, Silvery cassia

Dry to 9" year round. Low nutrient needs; mulch and compost will suffice. In climates with cool summers, thin plants in spring to increase air circulation and warm the soil; in hotter areas, pinch or shear plants in spring to induce bushiness and increase root shading. Feathery cassia produces lots of seeds; to reduce the mess and nuisance, shear plants again after bloom in late summer.

Tecoma stans Yellow bells or Yellow trumpet

Dry to 6" to 9" year round, depending on distance from coast and amount of shade. Moderate nutrient needs; a layer of mulch or compost along with a well-balanced organic supplement will be needed yearly. Deadheading in summer may encourage another bloom. Pinch or shear to contain and induce bushiness in winter. Remove damaged, crossing and rangy stems in late winter/early spring.

Trichostema lanatum Woolly blue curls

Southern California native from the chaparral plant community. Dry to 9" to 1' in winter and spring. No irrigation in summer and fall. Suffers from summer moisture. Low nutrient needs; nothing more than wood chips is needed. Good drainage is essential. Deadheading in late spring may spur another bloom in summer. Remove rangy and damaged stems in late fall/early winter. Often short-lived in urban areas.

Umbellularia californica California bay

Southern California native found in forests, along streams, and in canyons. Dry to 6" winter and spring, and to 1' summer and fall. Moderate nutrient needs; if not given a regular layer of mulch or compost, then organic fertilizers will be needed. Pinch or shear for compaction and containment anytime. Thin and remove rangy growth in late fall/ early winter. Prone to sooty mold, brought on by aphids and scale, which are encouraged by poor air circulation, overwatering and too much fertilizing.

Westringia fruiticosa Coast rosemary

Dry to 6" in spring, to 1' in summer and fall. No irrigation in winter. Low nutrient needs; wood chips, mulch or compost will suffice. Responds well to shearing and the plant can be hedged anytime. Remove rangy growth in winter through spring.

Plant Names

Low, Rooting and Spreading: Common Names to Botanical

Acacia, desert or carpet *Acacia redolens, A. r. 'Desert Carpet'*
Balearic Island sage *Phlomis italica*
California copperleaf *Acalypha californica*
California lilac, prostrate *Ceanothus gloriosus, C. griseus horizontalis,*
    C. maritimus
Chamise, prostrate *Adenostoma fasciculatum 'Prostrate'*
Cotoneaster, bearberry *Cotoneaster dammeri 'Lowfast'*
Coyote brush *Baccharis pilularis*

Creeping snowberry *Symphoricarpos albus, S. mollis*

Creeping St. Johnswort *Hypericum calycinum*

Indian hawthorn *Rhaphiolepis indica 'Ballerina'*

Junipers, prostrate *Juniperus* spp.

Lantana, purple trailing *Lantana montevidensis*

Mahonia: Oregon grape, desert mahonia, California holly grape, creeping mahonia *Berberis (Mahonia) aquifolium, B. fremontii, B. pinnata, B. repens*

Manzanita, trailing *Arctostaphylos* spp. 'Prostrate'

Mirror plant, creeping *Coprosma repens*

Myoporum, Pacific; creeping myoporum *Myoporum 'Pacificum', M. parvifolium*

Natal plum, prostrate *Carissa macrocarpa 'Green Carpet'*

Poverty weed or San Diego marsh-elder *Iva hayesiana*

Rosemary *Rosmarinus officinalis 'Prostratus'*

Silver sage *Artemisia 'Powis Castle'*

Silver spreader *Artemisia caucasica*

Low, Rooting and Spreading: Botanical Names to Common

Acacia redolens, A. r. 'Desert Carpet' Desert carpet

Acalypha californica California copperleaf

Adenostoma fasciculatum 'Prostrate' Prostrate chamise

Arctostaphylos spp. 'Prostrate' Trailing manzanita

Artemisia caucasica Silver spreader

Artemisia 'Powis Castle' Silver sage

Baccharis pilularis Coyote brush

Berberis (Mahonia) aquifolium, B. fremontii, B. pinnata, B. repens Oregon grape, desert mahonia, California holly grape, creeping mahonia

Carissa macrocarpa 'Green Carpet' Prostrate natal plum

Ceanothus gloriosus, C. griseus horizontalis, C. maritimus California lilac

Coprosma repens Creeping mirror plant

Cotoneaster dammeri 'Lowfast' Bearberry cotoneaster

Hypericum calycinum Creeping St. Johnswort

Iva hayesiana Poverty weed or San Diego marsh-elder

Juniperus spp. A variety of creeping / prostrate junipers

Lantana montevidensis Purple trailing lantana

Myoporum 'Pacificum', M. parvifolium Pacific myoporum and creeping myoporum

Phlomis italica Balearic Island sage

Rhaphiolepis indica 'Ballerina' Indian hawthorn

Rosmarinus officinalis 'Prostratus' Rosemary

Symphoricarpos albus, S. mollis Creeping snowberry

Larger Shrub: Botanical Names to Common

Abutilon palmeri Indian mallow

Acca sellowiana (Feijoa sellowiana) Pineapple guava

Alyogyne huegelii Blue hibiscus

Anisodontea xhypomandarum Cape mallow

Arctostaphylos spp. Manzanita

Artemisia spp. Wormwood and sagebrush

Buddleja spp. Butterfly bush

Caesalpinia pulcherrima Mexican poininciana or red bird of paradise

Calliandra californica, C. eriophylla Baja fairy duster and fairy duster

Carpenteria californica Bush anemone

Cercidium spp. Palo Verde

Cercocarpus spp. Mountain mahogany

Cistus spp. Rockrose

Correa spp. Australian fuchsia

Dalea spp. Indigo bush

Dasylirion spp. Mexican grass tree or desert spoon

Dendromecon harfordii, D. rigida Island bush poppy and bush poppy

Dodonaea spp. Hopseed

Encelia californica Bush sunflower and California encelia

Eriogonum spp. Buckwheat

Fallugia paradoxa Apache plume

Fremontodendron spp. Fremontia or flannel bush

Gambelia (Galvezia) speciosa Island bush snapdragon

Grevillea spp. Grevillea

Hamelia patens Firebush or Texas firecracker bush

Heteromeles arbutifolia Toyon

Hyptis emoryi Desert lavender

Isomeris arborea Bladderpod or California cleome

Justicia californica and J. spicigera Chuparosa and Mexican honeysuckle.

Keckiella spp. Heart leaved penstemon, chaparral beardtongue, climbing penstemon

Lantana spp. Lantana

Larrea tridentata Creosote bush

Lavandula spp. Lavender

Leonotis leonurus Lion's tail.

Leucadendron Cultivars, *L. discolor, L. tinctum* Leucadendron

Leucophyllum spp. Texas ranger

Malva (Lavatera) assurgentiflora, M. maritime Island mallow and tree mallow

Mimulus aurantiacus Sticky monkey flower

Morella (Myrica) californica Pacific wax myrtle

Perovskia spp. Russian sage

Phlomis fruticosa Jerusalem sage

Plumbago auriculata Cape plumbago

Prosopis spp. Mesquite

Prunus ilicifolia, P. i. lyonii Hollyleaf cherry and Catalina cherry

Quercus spp. Scrub oaks

Rhamnus (Frangula) californica, R. crocea Coffeeberry, redberry

Rhus spp. (Western natives only) Lemonade berry, pink flowering sumac, sugar bush

Ribes spp. Gooseberry and currant

Rosa californica California wild rose

Russelia equisetiformis Coral fountain

Salvia 'Allen Chickering', *S. apiana, S. Bee's Bliss, S. brandegei, S. canariensis, S. clevelandii, S.* 'Dara's Choice', *S. greggii, S. leucophylla, S. mellifera, S. microphylla* Allen Chickering sage, white sage, bee's bliss, Santa Rosa Island sage, Canary Island sage, Cleveland Sage, autumn sage, purple sage, black sage, cherry sage, Mrs. Beard sage

Santolina chamaecyparissus Lavender cotton

Senna artemisioides, C. phyllodinea Feathery cassia and silvery cassia

Tecoma stans Yellow bells or yellow trumpet

Trichostema lanatum Woolly blue curls

Umbellularia californica California bay

Westringia fruiticosa Coast rosemary

9

Succulents and Cactus

Southern California has had a long love affair with succulents and cacti. And it's no wonder. These plants provide dramatic statements, energizing colors, and exciting forms—all for low water and maintenance costs. There is a lot to love.

A succulent is a plant that actively stores water in its stem, leaves and roots. All cacti are succulents, but not all succulents are cacti. Cactus is distinguished from other succulents by its spines and hairs. Cactus spines grow in clumps, succulents do not. These clumps of spines and hairs are the places where new flowers and growth comes from; succulents do not bloom or grow in this manner.

As a general rule: succulents do better along the coast, where there is little danger of frost and freeze. Cactus does better inland, where there is less danger of moisture and rot. This chapter provides notes on individual plant care, which includes right type of soil, irrigation, mulches, fertilization, pruning, pests and propagation. Scientifically speaking, not every plant in this chapter is a succulent, but they've been included here because they are often treated like one.

Variegated blue agave, *Aloe arborescens,* blue chalk fingers (*Senecio mandraliscae*) and *Cotyledon orbiculata* (in the background) creates a dynamic landscape that requires little maintenance and water.

General Growing Tips

Below are general guidelines for growing succulents and includes information on soils, irrigation, mulches, fertilization, pruning, pests and propagation. Following this section are specific recommendations for individual succulents.

Soil

Good drainage is paramount to success. Succulents generally prefer gritty soils and suffer in too much clay. Most favor soils with neutral pH to slightly acidic (6 to 7 pH). Not surprisingly, many Southwestern succulents, like *Dudleya* and yucca, grow well in slightly alkaline soils. Succulents generally have low to moderate nutrient needs and dislike nutrient-rich, bacteria dominated soils.

If Too Sandy

Add organic material, the best being wood chips, mulch and compost. Avoid humus.

If Too Clayey

Add a combination of wood chips, grit (small gravel) and compost to at least 12". Other effective additives include gravel, mulch, perlite, pumice, and sharp sand.

Irrigation

Succulents are low-water plants—cactus even more so—but they are irrigated differently than other drought-adapted plants. While most have extensive roots, their roots are typically shallow. Succulents and cactus generally prefer a light watering at more frequent intervals. And, because of their extensive roots, make sure to irrigate beyond the plant's drip line. Importantly, do not irrigate during periods of high humidity.

Not all succulents/cacti need irrigation; however others will need it year round. Generally succulents do better along the coast and cactus inland.

Little to No Summer Water

Aeonium, Agave, Cotyledon, Dudleya, Escobaria, Ferocactus, Haworthia, Lemaire-ocereus, Nolina, Opuntia, Senecio, Yucca

No Winter Water

Aloe, Escobaria, Euphorbia, Ferocactus, Lemaireocereus, Opuntia

May Need Year Round Water

Beaucarnea, Bulbine, Calandrinia, Crassula, Dadyliron, Echeveria, Epiphyllum, Furcraea, Gasteria, Pachyphytum, Portulacaria, Sedum, Sempervivum

Quick Guide to Watering Succulents

- Do not water when foggy, overcast, or when there is high humidity.
- Water in the morning so the foliage can dry before night.
- If a succulent looks plump, colorful and juicy, it probably does not need water.
- If it looks listless, shriveled, or its leaves are bending downward, then it probably needs water.
- Rainwater is preferable because it is slightly acidic and soft and contains no salts and chemicals.

Signs of Overwatering

Leaves will show yellowish colors, translucent hues, and/or greyish tones.
Leaves and stems are swollen and split.
Insect and weed problems are prevalent.

Damage from overwatering is often irreversible; under-watering, generally not. Remedies include shutting off irrigation, pulling back mulches to expose and heat the soil, and pruning to increase sun exposure and airflow.

Many clues indicate this agave, sea fig, and coral tree are being overwatered; the leaves are too swollen, the leaf color is too rich, and the decomposed granite is water stained.

Mulches

Mulches reduce the need for irrigation. All mulches, including rock, reduce soil evaporation. However, organic mulches are not always best. If the area is in shade, high humidity, and near the coast, then organics can encourage rot and pest problems. Pea gravel, gravel, grit, river rock, sharp sand, and decomposed granite might be better options in these environments.

Chipped granite is used as mulch in this succulent garden along the coast. Newport Beach City Hall, Newport Beach.

Note: *The use of mulch can disguise overwatering. Allowing the soil to dry between watering is essential for healthy succulents and the look of mulch rarely offer clues to the condition of the soil. If mulch is used, then you will need to frequently scrap back the material to gauge soil moisture.* ■

Fertilization

Succulents need fertilizers infrequently in urban areas; cactus rarely ever. Urban soils are often nutrient-loaded from years of over-fertilization and decades of decaying roots. Even car exhaust, laden with vital nutrients (like nitrogen), contributes.

Typically, an application of wood chips, mulch or compost is needed yearly or every other year. If fertilizing with supplements, use a mild well-balanced fertilizer with equal amounts of nitrogen, phosphorous and potassium. A mixture of 3-3-3 is best. A good all-purpose organic fertilizer is 1 part blood meal, 1 part bone meal and 2 parts greensand. Spread 5lbs per 100sf.

Quick Fertilizing Tips

- Always water before fertilizing.
- Never fertilize a succulent during its dormant period (which could be winter or summer depending on the species).
- Never fertilize a sick or dry plant.
- Never fertilize directly after planting.
- It is always better to fertilize too little than too much.

Pruning

Pruning is vital to long-term health. It helps maintain air circulation, reduces overcrowding, and removes crossing stems and branches, all of which improves vigor and reduces pest problems.

Not all succulents and cacti need regular pruning, but some do. *Aeonium, Aloe, Agave, Euphorbia*, ice plant, *Opuntia, Portulacaria*, and *Senecio* will demand yearly attention. Dead material needs to be removed, the pups (vegetated starts) will have to be thinned and/or transplanted, and some succulents need constant containing.

The Monocarpic Group: There are many succulents that die after blooming. This group is called monocarpic. While an annual will do this in a year or less, an agave can take up to 100. The banana is the best known member of this unique group. Some of the most widely grown monocarpic succulents in Southern California are *Agave*, many *Aeoniums*, *Bromeliad*, *Furcraea*, and a couple of species of *Yucca*. As soon as a mono-carpic begins to bloom, plans for its replacement should begin.

Legginess: Some succulents get leggy with age. This is especially evident with *Aeonium* and *Echeveria*. These plants can become ugly as their trunks become long and lanky. Cut off the leafy sections 3" to 4" below the leaves, dry them for a week, and then replant the first 2" of the stems in the ground. Cut down the remaining trunk 1" from the ground. There's a 50% chance it will resprout. See Propagation below.

Dead and dying leaves have been removed, excess pups from the *Agave* pulled, and the *Aloe* has been pruned to keep it down. Energy Resource Center, Downey.

Dressing for Success

From long and barbed thorns to toxic sap, succulents have a slew of ways of torturing gardeners and landscapers. Come prepared. Wearing the right clothes will greatly reduce injury.

- Eye Protection: Eye protection is absolutely mandatory—the spines of *Agave*, *Opuntia* and *Yucca* are often hard to see, yet deadly. Goggles are best.

- Leather Gloves: Few materials offer the protection of leather. Thorns can't penetrate and sap can't seep through. If constantly working around these plants, invest in rose pruning gloves, which also protect most of the forearm.

- Long-Sleeved Shirt: A sturdy shirt will deter the most common injury— scraps and punctures along the arms. Naturally, the thicker the fabric, the greater the protection.

- Long Sturdy Pants: Only long pants will do—shorts offer little protection and skirts get caught up.

- Boots: Spines can easily penetrate the soles and sides of tennis shoes. Strong leather work-boots provide the greatest protection and confidence.

- Baseball Cap: Not only does the thick fabric provide protection from spines, but the cap's bill prevents the head from getting too close to the plant. Large shade hats can get caught.

Eye protection, long leather gloves, baseball cap, long-sleeved shirt, sturdy long pants, and tough shoes means that this gardener is serious about personal health.

Pests

Aphids, gophers, mealybugs, mites, nematodes, rabbits, rats, rot, scale, slugs, snails and thrips are the most common pests of succulents and cacti. However, grown in the right conditions, succulents and cacti are generally pest-free. Urban areas, unfortunately, rarely offer just the right conditions. Pests are more likely when a plant is overwatered, over-fertilized, the air is too humid or too still, and/or the plant is too coated in dust and urban grime. (Please refer to the chapter on Natural Pest Control for specific strategies).

Many of the natural strategies for controlling pests involve human contact, which is problematic for this group of plants because they often have adaptations that repel large mammals, which of course, includes us. Consequently, chemical insecticides—both contact and systemic— are frequently recommended. But, as it turns out, many of these chemicals create other problems. The oily chemicals increase chances of sunburn and the systemics can harm beneficial insects, including the plant's pollinator. For these reasons, chemical insecticides have limited success on succulents and cactus. The best defense is an effective offense—growing healthy plants.

Cochineal has a stranglehold on this pancake cactus. Some experts, though, claim that the scale-like insect deters other, more damaging pests, and may actually improve the health of *Opuntia* spp. in the long run.

Maintain Health for Pest Protection

- Do not overwater, or irrigate during times of high humidity.

- Do not fertilize unless there's a physical indicator that it is needed.

- Increase air circulation.

- Wash foliage.

- Take measures immediately; do not let a problem get a stranglehold.

Weeds

Succulent and cactus landscapes are ripe for urban weeds and there are always plenty. Succulents are generally not aggressive enough to out-compete weeds. Weeding these types of landscapes poses two problems. First, pulling weeds by hand can be treacherous to the gardener. Second, if herbicides come in contact with these plants, injury to the plants is likely as they are sensitive.

There are three strategies for weeding succulent landscapes: First, keep the first two inches of the soil as dry as possible. This minimizes opportunities for germination. Second, control the site's weeds before they set seed. Third, use a preemergent herbicide. These chemicals are practical for large plots of matting succulents, places where physically weeding can easily cause injury to the plant.

Ever the opportunist, spurge is a tenacious and common weed in succulent landscapes.

Propagation

Propagation rarely falls to the people maintaining commercial properties, community associations, or municipal landscapes, but succulents and cacti might change that. Propagating these plants is easy and economically viable. They require the last amount of time, resources, and expertise to propagate and have the highest success rate.

The timing of propagation is essential to success. Most succulents are winter dormant and the best time to propagate is in late winter/spring. Summer dormant succulents, such as *Aeonium, Haworthia, Sempervivum* and *Senecio,* are propagated in fall. Propagation is easiest when temperatures range from 65° to 75° F.

There are four quick ways to propagate: divisions, leaf starts, pups and stem cuttings.

Divisions

Much like clumping grasses, some succulents produce new growth from their base, growing outward. Of these, the most commonly divided succulents include *Bulbine* and *Sansevieria.*

As a Rule

1. Begin in cool weather.

2. Moisten soil to 1' deep; do not over saturate.

3. Dig up plant, starting 4" to 6" from the plant's base.

4. If not dividing immediately, moisten, cover and shade the roots.

5. Cut the clump in half or thirds with a sharp knife or pruning saw.

6. Plant the divisions immediately.

7. Moisten the soil to 1' deep.

8. If drainage is good, moisten soil twice a week; if dense, moisten only once a week.

9. Put on normal irrigation schedule in 4 weeks.

These aloe divisions were just potted.

Leaf Starts

Aeonium, Echeveria, Gasteria, Graptoveria, Haworthia, Kalanchoe, Opuntia and *Sempervivum* are some of the popular succulents that can be started by leaf cuttings.

As a Rule

1. Cut a leaf at its joint. If possible, make the cut at an angle to prevent water collecting on the parent plant.

2. Place leaf in warm dry location to heal the wound. Do not plant until callused, which for some of the larger cacti can take up to a month.

3. Once wound is callused, place cutting into rooting medium or soil deep enough to prevent the leaf from toppling over, typically about 2". The rooting medium should contain little organic material.

4. Irrigate to keep the soil just slightly moist.

5. The plant will root in 4 to 8 weeks and show the signs by new growth.

6. Move the plant to the field and begin normal irrigation.

Young pads cut from pancake cactus (*Opuntia*). The pads were then placed in a dry and shaded area to let the wounds callous over.

The callused end of the *Opuntia* pad 9 days after the cut.

Pups (Offsets)

Aeonium Agaves, Aloe, Cotyledon, Crassula, Echeveria, Furcraea, Gasteria, Haworthia, Sedum, Sempervivum and *Yucca* are the most popular succulents that produce vegetated starts (baby plants) at their bases. These pups can easily be pulled off and planted.

This blue agave has many pups that can be cut away and planted elsewhere on the property. At least one or two pups should be kept as soon as the monocarpic plant starts blooming because it will shortly die. Self Realization Temple and Gardens, Encinitas.

As a Rule

1. Pull or clip pups from parent plant.

2. Trim broken or damaged roots to ¾" of the crown.

3. Push the pups into soil or rooting medium.

4. Lightly water twice a week.

5. In 4 weeks the plant will have enough roots to either be moved or go on a normal irrigation schedule.

Stem Cuttings

Stems can easily be used to start new plants. Some of the plants started by stem cuttings are *Aeonium, Dudleya, Echeveria, Euphorbia,* ice plants, *Kalanchoe, Opuntia, Pedilanthus, Portulacaria, Sansevieria, Senecio, Sedum* and *Sempervivum.* Columnar cacti can be cut and rooted and treated much the same as stem cuttings.

As a Rule

1. Cut long stems, preferably young ones.

2. Cut stem into 5" sections (columnar cactus a foot or more).

3. Remove leaves from bottom 2".

4. If the stem doesn't have leaves, mark its top with a pen or small slash; cuttings will not root if planted upside down.

5. Place stems in dry, warm environment until the wounds callus over, about 2 to 10 days (although columnar cactus can take a month or more).

6. Once callused, plant the stem in the soil or rooting medium.

7. If the plant is dormant, wait to water until temperatures exceed 70°F.

8. Begin normal irrigation when plant is actively in the growing season.

This bed of *Aeonium* would be reinvigorated if the stems were cut and replanted.

Situations that Cause the Most Problems

- Poor Drainage
- Frost and Freeze
- Watering: Overwater or Underwatering
- Poor Air Circulation
- Hard Water
- Overcrowding
- Overhead Irrigation

Individual Plant Care

The plants below are listed by their botanic names. At the end of this chapter is a list of these plants by their common name.

Note: *Irrigation requirements are expressed in the amount of inches a soil should dry before receiving supplemental water. Naturally, if a soil never dries to prescribed depth, which is not uncommon during monsoons, then the plant requires no irrigation.* ■

Aeonium spp.

Ground covers to shrub size. Needs more water and nutrients than most succulents. Summer dormant. Although they remain attractive drying to 5" in summer, their dormant season, the rest of the year they look better and bloom more if they dry to only 3". Moderate nutrient needs; yearly application of mulch and compost may be needed. Some varieties are monocarpic and will die after flowering.

Agave spp.

Ground covers to large shrub size. Tough and durable plants. Can dry to 9" throughout the year, but are more attractive if they only dry to 6" in summer. Low nutrient needs; nothing more than wood chips, mulch and gravel are needed. Monocarpic. Propagate from profuse pups.

Aloe spp.

Ground covers to tree-height. Tough. Can grow in nearly every Southern California garden, but they are not as drought tolerant as some other succulents. Dry to 4" in spring, 6" in summer and fall. No irrigation in winter. Moderate nutrient needs; mulch, compost and/or diluted balanced organic fertilizers will be needed. Propagate from pups, and stem and leaf cuttings. Prune, propagate and plant late winter/early spring.

Beaucarnea spp. Ponytail Palm, Elephant's Foot

Tree size. Beaucarnea can dry to 6", but be aware that can happen quickly because of the plant's size and also the coarse soil required to grow it well. Along the coast it may not need irrigation winter through early spring. Too much water creates lackluster growth and a variety of pest problems. Low to moderate nutrient needs; only wood chips, mulch and compost are needed.

Bulbine spp.

Ground covers to low shrub size. Summer dormant. Although bulbine can survive with little water, it has better year round appearance if soil never dries to more than 4". Low nutrient needs; wood chips, mulch and compost should suffice. Divide and plant in fall/early winter.

Calandrinia grandiflora, C. spectabilis Rock purslane

Shrub size. Tough. Can tolerate drought and poor soils, but looks much better when only drying to 4" between waterings. Moderate nutrient needs and will grow well with nothing more than yearly mulch or compost, although a well-balanced organic fertilizer may improve the appearance of the foliage. Prune and plant winter/early spring.

Cotyledon spp.

Ground covers. Dry to only 3" in summer, but 4" to 6" the rest of the year. If in shade, it only requires irrigation in summer. Avoid overhead watering because it washes off attractive and protective white power. Low nutrient needs; nothing more than wood chips, mulch and compost are needed. Prune, propagate and plant in late winter/spring.

Crassula spp.

Ground covers to shrub size. Although tough, and can dry up to 6" throughout the year, they look better if they never dry to more than 4" in summer. Low nutrient needs; mulch and compost will suffice. Easy to propagate and plant in late winter/spring. A few varieties are monocarpic.

Cylindropuntia spp. Cholla

Shrub to tree size. Incredibly hardy in the deserts of Southern California. Dry to 1' in spring and summer. No irrigation the rest of the year. High humidity will kill this plant. Low nutrient needs; nothing more than a light layer of gravel and wood chips is needed. Prune, propagate and plant in late winter/early spring.

Dasylirion spp. Mexican grass tree, desert spoon. Refer to chapter on Shrubs.

Dracaena draco Dragon tree

Tree size. Drought-adapted. Dries to 6" year around, but, unlike a majority of the other plants in this chapter, Dragon Tree needs deep irrigation—to 2'. Moderate nutrient needs; compost, humus and well-balanced organic supplements may be needed yearly. The dragon tree prefers slightly acidic soils. A slow grower and more water and fertilizer will not speed the plant.

Dudleya spp. Liveforevers

Ground covers. Like a true Southern California native, *Dudleya* likes its moisture in the winter and spring. Along the coast dry to 4" during winter/spring and 1' in summer; if inland, dry to 4" winter/spring, and 6" summer. No irrigation in fall either along the coast or inland. Exceptionally low nutrient needs; nothing more than a light layer of gravel and wood chips are necessary. Propagate from pups and leaf cuttings in late winter/early spring.

Echeveria spp.

Ground covers. One of the few succulents that grows better with regular water and rich soil. Dry to 2" to 4" summer through fall, depending on distance from coast, and 6" to 9" winter through spring. Moderate nutrient needs; because of its matting nature, liquid fertilizers and concentrated organics powders, such as a mix of animal meals, are best. Prune, divide, propagate and plant late winter/early spring.

Escobaria spp. Pincushion cactus

Low growers to shrub size. Exceptionally drought tolerant. Dries to a 1'. Will rot in anything but gravelly soils. Low nutrient needs. Does well in slightly alkaline soils.

Euphorbia spp.

Ground covers to tree size. A spring and summer grower, it dries to 4" during those seasons, and to 6" in fall. No irrigation in winter. Low to moderate nutrient needs; yearly compost and mild well-balanced organic fertilizers may be required. Prune, propagate and plant in late winter.

Ferocactus spp. Barrel cactus

Shrub size. Incredibly tough. Dry to 1' or more in summer. No irrigation the rest of the year. Needs very sharp drainage—anything less than gravelly soil will kill it. Exceptionally low nutrient needs; wood chips, used sparingly, is all that is needed. Weeds and weeding are a problem in urban areas.

Fouquieria splendens Ocotillo

Shrub size. Ocotillos are monsoon-adapted. They should dry to no more than 6" in the spring and summer. No irrigation the rest of the year. Suffers greatly in clay soils. Low nutrient needs; wood chips and mulch are sufficient. Plant in fall and winter.

Furcraea foetida Mauritius hemp

Large shrub size. Dry to 6" along coast but to only 3" in hot inland areas. Moderate nutrient needs; compost and well-balanced organic supplements may be needed occasionally. Monocarpic. Plant in late fall/winter. Salt sensitive which will be evident from brown-edged leaves. Sunburns and blanches if grown in a sunny area too far inland. Propagate from pups in early spring.

Gasteria spp.

Ground cover. Tough plants but not as drought-tolerant as some other succulents. Dry to 3" throughout spring and summer, 4" to 5" in fall. No irrigation in winter. Low nutrient needs; wood chips, mulch, and compost will suffice. Prune, propagate and plant late winter/early spring. If leaves are discolored and plant looks listless, it is likely receiving too much sun. Replace and/or relocate to shadier spot.

Graptopetalum paraguayense Ghost plant

Ground covers. Summer grower. Dry to 6" in spring and fall, 3" to 4" in summer. No irrigation in winter. Moderate nutrient needs; compost and well-balanced organic supplements may be required every other year. Apply in early spring. Propagate by pushing wayward stems into the soil in late fall/winter. Plant in early spring.

Graptoveria spp.

Ground covers. Summer grower. Dries to 4" in summer, 6" in spring and fall. No winter irrigation. Moderate nutrient needs; mulch and a light well-balanced organic fertilizer may be needed early spring yearly. Propagate and plant late winter/early spring. Can be propagated by leaf and stem cuttings.

Haworthia

Ground covers. Summer dormant. Can dry to 1' during that time of year, but only to 4" in winter and spring. No irrigation in winter. Low nutrients needs. However, because of its dense matting nature, a well-balanced organic liquid may be needed occasionally. Favors a little shade and will show signs of sunburn if it is not provided. Propagate and plant in late fall/winter.

Hesperaloe spp. False yucca, Red yucca, Giant yucca

Shrub size. Drought-adapted. Only needs irrigation during the summer months, dry to 6". No irrigation the rest of the year. One of the few succulents to tolerate clay soils, but the soil must absolutely dry between waterings. Low to moderate nutrient needs; all that is required is yearly mulch or compost. Deadhead early summer. Plant in late winter/early spring.

Kalanchoe spp.

Ground covers to almost tree size. Tropical, but tough. Dry to only 4" in summer, but 6" in spring and fall. No irrigation during winter. Low to moderate nutrient needs (depending on species); mulches will be needed, plus an occasional well-balanced organic supplement. Prune, propagate and plant late fall/winter.

Nolina spp. Beargrass

Shrub size. A tough group with many species native to the southeastern part of Southern California. Dry to at least 6" spring and summer. No irrigation fall and winter. Low nutrient needs; a light layer of gravel and wood chips will do. Can rot along the coast. Plant in late winter/spring.

Opuntia spp. Pancake cactus, Prickly pear

Shrub to almost tree size. A coastal group of plants that thrive in gravelly soil and maritime moisture. Along the coast dry to 6" in spring, to 1' in summer. No irrigation in fall and winter. In the hotter inland areas dry to 4" in spring, 6" in summer. No irrigation fall or winter. Low nutrient needs; wood chips and mulch will do. A strand that is too dense or has too much dead material is more likely to have pest problems; periodic cleaning and rejuvenation is essential. Prune, propagate and plant in late fall/winter.

Pedilanthus spp. Slipper plant

Shrub size. Tough and durable. Dry to 1' in spring and summer along the coast, to 6" inland. No irrigation in fall or winter. Low nutrient needs; wood chips are all that is needed. Prone to rot in moist soils and climates. Prone to sunburn inland. Plant in late winter/early spring.

Portulacaria afra Elephant food

Shrub height. Tough and durable. Dry to 6" in spring and summer, and, if along the coast or in shade, needs no irrigation the rest of the year. Dry to 1' in fall and winter in the hotter interior. Low nutrient needs; wood chips and mulch will do. Prune to contain, improve structure and increase air circulation in late winter/early spring. Propagate and plant in winter through spring.

Sansevieria spp. Snake plant or Mother-In-law's tongue
Low shrub size. Durable. Can dry to 4" in spring and summer, 6" in fall. No irrigation in winter. Low to moderate nutrient needs; compost is usually all that is needed, but liquid organic concentrates are typically used because this plant is rarely placed in areas compatible to composts. Can sunburn inland. Divide and plant in late winter/spring.

Sedum spp. Stonecrop
Mostly ground covers, but some to shrub size. Although aggressive and successful in urban areas, they are not as drought adapted as other succulents. Dry to only 4" throughout the year for best results. Moderate nutrient needs; mulch, compost and well-balanced organic supplements may be needed yearly. Prune, propagate and plant late in late winter/early spring.

Sempervivum spp. Houseleek, Hens and chicks
Ground covers. Winter growers and summer dormant. Soil should not dry to more than 4" in late fall through early spring. Can dry to 6" in summer. Moderate nutrient needs; compost and well-balanced organic supplements may be needed yearly. Prune, propagate and plant in late fall/early winter.

Senecio mandraliscae, S. serpens Blue chalk fingers
Rooting ground cover. Winter grower. Soil can dry to 6" in summer and fall, but only 4" in spring. Dry to 6" or more in shade. No irrigation in winter. Moderate feeders; compost and a light well-balanced organic supplement every other year may improve appearance. Prune, propagate and plant in late fall/early winter.

Senecio spp.
Ground covers to shrubs and perennials. Winter growers. Soil can dry to 6" year around. Moderate feeders; compost and a light well-balanced organic supplement may be needed yearly. Prune, propagate and plant in late fall/early winter.

Yucca spp. Yucca
Low shrub to tree size. Several varieties are native to Southern California. One of the toughest group of succulents. Dry to 1' during summer. May not need irrigation the rest of the year. Low nutrient needs; only a layer of gravel or wood chips is needed. Pull dead leaves from the trunk and deadhead mid-summer. *Y. whipplei* is the only Yucca that dies after blooming (monocarpic).

Ice Plants

Ice plants are different from other trailing succulents. They are a Mesemb. All have daisy-like flowers, and a majority spread and root. Mesembs can be aggressive and have migrated to natural areas. Some varieties accumulate salts and will create a toxic environment to other plants over time. Mesembs are generally avoided.

If Mesembs are already planted, they prefer a consistent level of moisture throughout the year. They do best when irrigation is light but frequent. They can absorb moisture through their leaves and should never be irrigated in times of high humidity, no matter the temperature. Drainage is essential for all succulents and Mesembs favor gritty and gravelly soils low in digestible nutrients. While they do best is soils with neutral pH, they will tolerate a range if the drainage is good.

Mesembs includes the following species: *Aptenia cordifolia* (red apple), *Cephalophyllum* (red spike ice plant), *Delosperma* spp., *Drosanthemum* spp. (rosea ice plant), *Lampranthus* spp. (trailing ice plant), *Malephora* spp. (Croceum ice plant).

Common Names to Botanical

Aeonium spp.
Agave spp.
Aloe spp.
Barrel cactus *Ferocactus*
Beargrass *Nolina* spp.
Blue chalk fingers *Senecio mandraliscae, S. serpens*
Bulbine spp.
Cotyledon spp.
Cholla *Cylindropuntia* spp.
Crassula spp.
Croceum ice plant *Malephora crocea*
Dragon tree *Dracaena draco*
Echeveria spp.
Elephant food *Portulacaria afra*
Euphorbia spp.
Gasteria spp.
Ghost plant *Graptopetalum paraguayense*
Hesperaloe spp.
Haworthia spp.

Houseleek, Hens and chicks *Sempervivum* spp.

Ice plant *Delosperma* spp.

Kalanchoe spp.

Liveforevers *Dudleya* spp.

Mauritius hemp *Furcraea foetida*

Ocotillo *Fouquieria splendens*

Pancake cactus, Prickly pear *Opuntia* spp.

Pincushion cactus *Escobaria* spp.

Ponytail palm, Elephant's foot tree *Beaucarnea* spp.

Red apple *Aptenia cordifolia*

Red spike ice plant *Cephalophyllum*

Rock purslane *Calandrinia grandiflora, C. spectabilis*

Rosea ice plant *Drosanthemum* 'Red Spike'

Slipper plant *Pedilanthus* spp.

Snake plant or mother-In-law tongue *Sansevieria* spp.

Stonecrop *Sedum* spp.

Trailing ice plant *Lampranthus* spp.

Yucca spp.

PART IV

Pests

10

Weed Control

Southern California is fertile. Weeds love it here. Weeding is the most frequent job in our gardens by far, and we chop, pull and spray for a variety of reasons. We weed to maintain aesthetic integrity, ensure that the water and fertilizers we give to a landscape goes to the plants we select, and help plants and landscapes fulfill their designated functions, such as shading, erosion control or food production.

This chapter is built around the three phases of weed control: prevention, protection and eradication. Prevention stops unwanted plants from getting onto property. Protection stops unwanted plants from either sprouting or spreading on a property. And eradication involves all the techniques and tools used to physically remove weeds.

PREVENTION   **PROTECTION**   **ERADICATION**

Weeds occupy particular niches, and understanding them helps the gardener understand the animals, insects and processes that are interacting with the landscape. Weeds are also a good way to read soil conditions. At the end of this chapter is a list of weeds and the conditions each prefers.

Prevention

Prevention helps stop weeds from either travelling onto a property or germinating on a property. The techniques used to prevent weeds from spreading are ensuring no weeds onsite go to seed, putting up barriers to the migration of seeds, cleaning equipment that travels between properties, and going beyond property lines to tackle offsite sources of weeds.

No Seeds Onsite

It is okay to let weeds grow for a while; in fact, sometimes it can even be beneficial. Weeds help break up dense soil, enrich poor soil, and attract pollinators. It is never okay, however, to let weeds go to seed. Letting weeds produce seed guarantees next year's crop will be larger.

If the weeds are high, such as grasses, mow or weed-whack them before they go to seed. If the weeds are low, such as bindweed and spurge, scrap them off the soil. The timing of this task hinges on observation. The goal is to cut back after the plant has flowered but before it has set seed.

Barriers

Weed seeds are designed to travel. They flit and tumble down streets and sidewalks; hitch rides on birds and lizards; and catch air currents, take flight and soar above shrubs and trees. Barriers help block this constant migration.

Vegetative Barrier

Whether 1' tall or 10', vegetation is fantastic at pulling seeds and particulates out of the air. The most effective plants have key characteristics: leaves are small but the plant is dense; leaves are sticky or oily; and leaves are more stiff than flexible. Some of the best barrier plants include arborvitae, *Ceanothus*, coyote brush, cypress, juniper, *Justicia*, lantana, lavender, myrtle, rockrose, rosemary, *Santolina*, sumac, *Teucrim*, and *Westringia*.

A low hedge of rosemary has visibly trapped debris and weed seeds from blowing on to the property.

Barrier Wall

Whether a small wall or tall fence, any type of barrier affects wind patterns and the places where weed seeds get deposited.

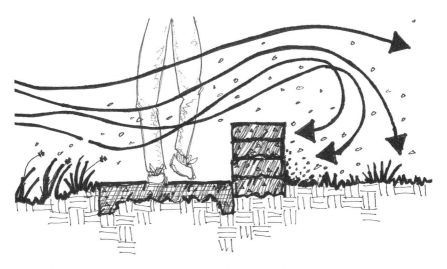

A small barrier can help reduce the amount of weed seeds being blown across a property. As wind rushes over a small wall a wind eddy is created, causing the wind to circle behind the wall and deposit its seeds and debris.

Clean Travelling Gear

Boots, edgers, mowers, tarps, tires and weed-whackers are some of the ways people unwittingly transport weed seeds between properties. If going from a particularly weedy property to one that is well maintained, quickly cleaning machinery and gear is a high priority. A blast of air from a compressor is a quick substitute for using water.

Look Beyond the Property

Simply putting up barriers and weeding your own property may not be enough to stop the constant migration of weed seeds. Sometimes your efforts will be needed in the landscapes outside of your own. Removing weeds from adjacent properties or creating a buffer zone around your own property can reduce the amount of time needed to weed your own landscape.

Protection

Providing protection helps stop weeds from either germinating or spreading. The techniques used to protect a landscape from weed seeds include planting aggressive plants and laying down mulches, and in the worst case, using a weed barrier as a short-term solution.

Weed Truisms

Southern California has no problem growing weeds. This abundance creates two inescapable truisms:

1. You either pick your weeds or they pick you.

Weeds flourish when they don't have competition. Any small patch of bare soil is a opportunity. One of the most successful strategies for weed control is planting plants that can outcompete the weeds. Instead of letting birds or wind currents determine which weeds will dominate an area, the gardener chooses the plants that will dominate. The landscaping plants, in essence, become the weeds. Below is a more detailed discussion on aggressive plants.

2. You either have to prune a lot or weed a lot.

Landscapes that require little weeding because of the aggressive plants that dominate it generally need more pruning. Some ground covers, like primrose, sundrops and wild strawberry, are incredibly effective at weed suppression, but they need constant corralling. Always budget time for one of the two— weeding or pruning.

Some types of landscapes struggle to keep weeds at bay. In the case of this succulent landscape the increase in weeding is offset by the decrease in pruning and cleaning.

The star jasmine pictured is a good example of a pruning landscape. This rooting vine has suppressed weeds in this bed for over eight years. The tradeoff is an increase in pruning. Containing the plant is necessary once a month.

Use Aggressive Plants

The best defense is often a strong offense. Using plants that can out-compete weeds is one of the greatest time-savers in maintaining a landscape. The plants most likely to beat weeds share some general characteristics:

- They trail and root across the top of the soil.
- They are self-repairing and spring back from injury.
- Their foliage blocks the sun from striking the soil.
- They may have aggressive roots near the surface that hog water and nutrients.
- They may be prolific seeders.

Many of the plants listed in the *Low-Growing and Rooting* sections of the Perennial and Shrub chapters are aggressive enough to outcompete weeds. Some of the plants that can be seeded, and then reseed prolifically on their own, are alyssum, baby blue eyes, blue-eyed grass, California poppy, *Clarkia*, forget-me-nots, golden yarrow, goldfields, *Silene*, tidy tips, and yarrow.

Santa Barbara Daisy *(Erigeron karvinskianus)* can be an aggressive spreader and successfully out-compete a variety of weeds.

Mulches

Controlling weeds by using mulches is a universally recommended method of control. Mulch suppresses growth by blanketing existing weeds and preventing incoming seeds from touching soil and rooting. Mulches can be divided between organic or inorganic.

Organic Mulches

Not all mulches are equally effective at suppressing weeds. Finely decomposed mulches are great for growing plants, but not for weed suppression. Recently chipped plant material is great for weed protection, but not for nourishing plants (at least not initially). Recently chipped material from plants high in oils typically offers the best suppression. Wood chips of this sort can chemically inhibit germination, bind soils, and help to slow fast-moving water.

The most effective mulches for weed suppression are recently chipped *Acacia*, camphor, *Eucalyptus*, juniper, oak, pine and *Pittosporum*. Large, thick mulches are preferred over fine, thin mulches.

Thick, woody and coarse mulch will help suppress weeds until the shrubs, grasses and succulents in this landscape mature. Irvine Valley College, Irvine.

Inorganic Mulches

Inorganic mulches, such as decomposed granite, gravel and river rock, can help suppress weeds, but do not get rid of them. The biggest benefit of using inorganic mulch is the ease of eradicating weeds. Whatever weeding method you use—be it flaming pulling, scraping or spraying, inorganic mulches can make the task easier.

River rock mulch

That said, decomposed granite—the popular mulch and path material—has some drawbacks as a weed suppressant. First, it is the perfect rooting medium for many weeds, so they might increase in number. Second, the increase in weeds increases the number of people walking on the mulch to control them. And third, decomposed granite compacts easily under human weight, which then creates a mulch that is quick to produce runoff, but slow to allow the soil to exchange its gases, which then leads to diminishing plant health. For these reasons, decomposed granite is not universally recommended; pea gravel or small rock chips are usually more effective.

Unless DG has been treated with a binding agent or compacted, it will attract weeds. It has neutral pH, is disease free, and creates just enough air space for rooting. Pictured above is a young crop of horseweed and spurge.

Mulching For Success

Follow these tips to get the greatest impact from your mulching endeavors:

- Keep all mulches away from the crown of plants. Smothering the crown can lead to rot and death.

- Avoid fine mulches for weed suppression because they break down too quickly.

- Spread nothing less than a 2" layer of material if trying to suppress weeds, a 4" layer is better.

- Beware of giving too much organic mulch to tough Mediterranean plants. Organics provide nutrients and overtime routinely mulched areas can become too rich to favor plants adapted to nutrient poor environments.

- Only use thick, compactable organic mulches in fire hazard areas. Fine mulches, like gorilla hair, are much too ignitable.

- Always examine the soil before irrigating mulched areas. Mulches have a tendency to make an area look dry, even if the soil is wet.

Weed Fabric/Barriers

Weed barriers are short-term solutions only. Cardboard, newspaper, plastic sheets and weed fabric are laid over soil to prevent underlying weeds from sprouting. Usually a thick layer of mulch is laid over these materials. These materials are highly effective in the short-term. However in the long-term these materials can increase maintenance costs. Weed barriers can be divided between organic and inorganic types.

Organic: Organic materials, such as cardboard and mulch, will certainly smother the weeds that lay beneath them. Over time, though, organics break down and provide an ideal environment for a greater range of weeds, including some that are more aggressive. Organic barriers are an excellent way to prepare an area for future planting, but they are not good for long-term weed suppression.

Inorganic: Plastic sheets and weed fabrics are commonly sold as solutions to weed problems, and, for the first two years, they can be. But over time a fine layer of organic debris accumulates on their surfaces and weed seeds begin sprouting in this layer. Some of these roots will pierce the weed barriers, quickly rooting and growing. Now pulling or chopping the weed involves dealing with this fabric or plastic. Once these materials reach the surface there is little success in pushing them back down. Landscape fabric and plastic sheeting are ideal for separating different materials, such as river rock and soil, but as an effective weed barrier they are only good in the short-term.

Landscape fabric eventually becomes a landscape nuisance. Unless it is biodegradable, it is often better to avoid weed-blocking fabrics.

Eradication

Removing weeds is never an easy task, and there is no easy way to do it. However the methods listed below have proven to be the most effective. Know, though, that simply yanking out a weed does not mean it has been controlled. In some situations that action can actually increase weeds, because it sows the next crop. Follow the suggestions below to get the most out of weeding time.

Most Common Weeding Mistakes

■ Weeding after the plants have set seeds only sows the next crop. Instead, always try to weed before seed production.

■ Spraying weeds with an herbicide before pulling them makes the task harder because dead plants are more prone to breakage. Instead, pull the weeds, let the remaining seeds and shoots sprout, and then either pull those or use a herbicide.

■ Weeding when the soil is wet not only makes the task dirtier, it compacts the soil as well, undermining soil and plant health. Instead, wait until the area is only slightly moist before weeding.

■ Weeding a massive infestation without a plan to come back in a month is a waste of time because there is always an immediate crop afterwards. Quick-growing weeds will set seed in 4 to 6 weeks. Without controlling this second surge of weeds the infestation will bounce right back. Instead, always plan to weed an infestation at least twice, about 4 weeks apart.

Protect Ecological Health

Everything coexists in a garden—bacteria and bugs, plants and animals—everything, including us. Hurt one and the others are damaged as well. Great care should be taken to minimize injury to these vital residents when weeding. Protect plants from falling and dragged debris. Lay boards and plywood over beds, grasses and soils to distribute the weight of repeated footsteps. If working in dry conditions, apply a light watering to help bind the soil and reduce topsoil loss. And never, ever, work in wet soils because of the oxygen-squeezing compaction it causes.

Chopping / Mowing

Tools: Brush-cutter, machete, sickle, weed-whacker

Best Plant(s): Any plant with a trunk diameter of 1" or less.

Timing: Though it is easier to mow in mid-spring when plants are tender, most professionals wait until just before the plant has set seed, ensuring the services of the plant without the burden of its offspring the following year.

Note: Chopping and mowing increases soil compaction, which in turn changes infiltration rates, gas exchange rates, and plant health. A good land manager will minimize the frequency of mowing by maximizing its impact through proper timing. Get to know the reproduction cycles of the plants you are trying to control.

Equipment and Fire

According to the California Department of Forestry the leading cause of wild-fires is equipment use. Mowers, weed-whackers and chainsaws are a constant source of friction, heat and sparks. To avoid starting a fire while working with machinery, the following precautions should be taken:

- Bring a fire extinguisher to the work site.
- Put spark arresters on all exhaust ports and repair holes in existing systems.
- Never lay a running or hot engine in grass or other ignitable vegetation.
- Check for a build-up of carbon in exhaust system and on spark plugs.
- Refuel only when the engine has cooled down.
- Avoid working past 10 am during the fire season.
- Avoid all work that involves machinery during extreme fire weather, those hot, dry and windy days.

Digging

Tools: Hand trowel, shovel, pry bar

Best Plant(s): Large grasses, plants with rhizomes, medium-sized shrubs.

Timing: Preferably late winter/early spring, when the soils are moist and pliable and the weeds have not set seed.

Note: Digging up a plant will scar and excite the seeds within the soil, increasing both weeds immediately and the following spring. Always plan to come back to control that first big surge of weeds.

Herbicides

Tools: Large array of chemicals

Best Plant(s): Plants under 2'. Whether applied as a contact, systemic, or preemergent, herbicides are effective against smaller plants. The exception to this general rule is controlling resprouting shrubs and trees. Dousing a freshly cut stump with a systemic non-selective herbicide will prevent it from resprouting.

Timing: Effectiveness depends on the material being used and the plant it is being used on. Even if the material is organic, read instructions carefully before applying. Never, ever, use a herbicide when it is rainy or windy.

Note: Chemical herbicides have advantages. They can be incredibly effective and they are not as disruptive as some of the other methods, such as digging and scraping. However, their long-term biological, cultural and public health costs can be significant. As a rule, herbicides are only used if the other prevention, protection and eradication strategies fail to work. Legally, an herbicide's label must be read before using.

The Bradley Method of Control

Is your landscape overrun by a large infestation of weeds? If so, try the Bradley Method. In this method the outlying, less infested areas are tackled first. This creates a greater chance that the plants you want to thrive and outcompete the weeds will be successful. Once the smaller, less infested areas are controlled, then, and only then, move on to the more severely impacted areas.

—*Invasive Plants of California's Wildlands*. Edited by Carla C. Bossard, John M. Randelland, Marc C. Husbovsky. University of California Press. 2000. p. 21.

Plowing / Tilling

Tools: Shovel, rototiller, tractor

Best Plant(s): Fleshy and young plants and roots.

Timing: Preferably before plants set seed.

Note: As a method of weed control tilling is a short-lived solution because it sows the next crop of weeds. While tilling crops, such as green manures, into a soil will enhance fertility, turning over soil without vegetative cover will degrade the soil, killing beneficial microbes and reducing fertility.

Pulling

Tools: Strong back and hands. Devices such as pry bars and weed-wrenches help, too.

Best Plant(s): Although, technically, any plant is a candidate, young plants are the easiest to pull.

Timing: Pliable, semi-moist and warming spring soils are the easiest to weed by hand. As a rule, the majority of weeds should be pulled before they have set seed because pulling sows seeds.

Note: Weeding by hand can increase soil compaction. Mulch regularly to reduce impact.

Scraping

Tools: Hand hoe, shovel, sod cutter, bulldozer, weed-whacker

Best Plant(s): Anything under a ¾" diameter is a candidate; the smaller the stem or trunk, the easier the job.

Timing: Scraping is easiest when plants are fleshy and growing, rather than brittle, dormant or dead. Spring is generally a good time. Never scrap dry, rocky landscapes near flammable vegetation during the fire season: scraping produces sparks.

Note: Scraping is quick and effective, but can remove or injure topsoil. If scraping is repetitive, then maintain a layer of organic mulch over the area. Scraping is especially effective on decomposed granite surfaces.

Smothering / Sheet Mulching

Tools: Smothering works by creating a barrier that the plants below cannot grow through. Materials used for smothering include cardboard, newspaper and landscape fabrics, all of which are protected by a layer of mulch about 4" thick. Mulch used by itself should be at least 6" thick.

Best Plant(s): Low growing annuals, biennials and perennials.

Timing: Mid-winter through late spring is the best time. The goal is to smother the plants during their growing season; there is little benefit in blanketing a dormant plant.

Note: Smothering is effective. It works against the plants and seeds already onsite and helps deter incoming seeds from rooting. However, the benefits of smothering rarely last longer than 2 years, at which point the soil may be more fertile and hospitable to a greater range of weeds.

Solarization

Tools: Rolls of clear plastic sheets and staples for the plastic. The goal with solarization is to cook the plants and soils below, killing plants, vegetative starts and seeds.

Best Plant(s): Low-growing annuals, biennials and perennials.

Timing: Solarization works best in the hotter months, late spring through mid-fall. The process of sterilization can take 1 to 3 months. Clear an area of vegetation before laying plastic so that the sheets can lie directly on the soil.

Notes: Solarization solves an immediate problem and can be effective at preparing an area for future planting. Its drawbacks are the length of time it takes, the fact it requires lots of plastic which is only used once, and its ineffectiveness in areas that are cool and/or shady.

Vinegar

Tools: Vinegar, undiluted or diluted with water up to 50%. Vinegar is an acidic solution that kills vegetative cells on contact.

Best Plant(s): Fleshy, green plants; twiggy, woody plants are not as susceptible.

Timing: Vinegar works best late winter to mid-spring when weeds are young and fleshy.

Notes: Vinegar only kills what it touches and will not kill the roots of re-sprouting weeds, like Bermuda grass.

Handling Weed Waste

Removing weeds often entails removing large piles of debris. There are three ways to remove weed waste: compost on site, burn or haul away.

Composting is an inexpensive method, but it requires the greatest amount of time and space. Weed waste needs the most extensive type of composting to ensure that the vegetative starts and seeds are dead. A site's ability to properly compost also hinges on its ability to absorb the product.

Burning is the quickest and least expensive method, but is not legal in the urban areas of Southern California. Burning used to be the most common method of disposal, but because of our region's air quality mandates not any more.

Hauling the debris is the most expensive method of removal, but it is the quickest, by far. The expense of hauling is related to weight and size, both of which will shrink if the pile is spread out and allowed to dry before hauling away.

What are the Weeds Telling You About Your Soil?

Below is a list of weeds and the soils they prefer. It is a good starting point for your observation and understanding. Along with decades of personal observation, this list was created with help from CalFlora's comprehensive catalog (www.calflora.org) and the extensive work of University of California, Agriculture and Natural Resources, Statewide Integrated Pest Management Program (www.ipm.ucdavis.edu).

A California Friendly landscape would rarely create the conditions that favor nutgrass (*Cyperus* spp.). This weed prefers moist and slightly acidic soils. In the situation pictured above the mulch should be scrapped off to warm the soil and the irrigation should be severely turned down.

Barley (*Hordeum* spp.)

Indicates: Dry, shallow soil, with some salt and low fertility. Many California natives.

Berry, black or rasp (*Rubus* spp.)

Indicates: Acidic soil with salts, low fertility, and the soil might be shallow. Prefers shade with a moist spring and dry summer. Some California natives.

Bermuda grass (*Cynodon dactylon*)
Indicates: Dry soil that might also be acidic with low salts.

Bindweed (*Convolvulus* spp.)
Indicates: Low nutrients and shallow soil; might also be acidic.

Black medic (*Medicago lupulina*)
Indicates: Slightly moist soils with low nutrients and nitrogen.

Brome, ripgut (*Bromus diandrus*)
Indicates: Dry, disturbed and shallow soils with some fertility and salt.

Cape ivy (*Delairea odorata* (*Senecio mikaniodes*))
Indicates: Shady moist areas with soils that are neutral pH or slightly acidic.

Carrot, wild (*Daucus pusillus*)
Indicates: Dry soils with low fertility that might be slightly alkaline. California native.

Castor bean (*Ricinus communis*)
Indicates: Dry, disturbed, and shallow soils with low fertility that might also be acidic with some salt.

Cheeseweed (*Malva parviflora*)
Indicates: Dry, slightly infertile, and disturbed soils that might be low in salts.

Chickweed (*Stellaria media*)
Indicates: Slightly moist soils with low fertility that might also be compacted.

Chicory (*Cichorium intybus*)
Indicates: Dry soils that might have some salts and a pH that is neutral to slightly acidic.

Cinquefoil, creeping (*Potentilla reptans*)
Indicates: Acidic and slightly moist soils.

Clover, red, rose, white (*Trifolium* spp.)
Indicates: Low to moderate levels of moisture, low fertility and nitrogen, and soil that might also be acidic; some clovers also indicate high levels of potassium.

Cockleburr (*Xanthium* spp.)
Indicates: Dry, shallow soils that might have salt. California native.

Cow parsnip (*Heracleum maximum*)
Indicates: A shady or cool area with dry, acidic, shallow soils with low fertility and some salts.

Crabgrass (*Digitaria* spp.)
Indicates: Soils that are dry with low to moderate fertility and some compaction.

Dandelion (*Taraxacum officinale*)
Indicates: Acidic, slightly moist, and the soil be might be compacted but deep.

Dichondra (*Dichondra micrantha*)
Indicates: Moist, fertile and slightly acidic soils.

Dock (*Rumex* spp.)
Indicates: Moist, acidic soils that may be slightly infertile.

English daisy (*Bellis perennis*)
Indicates: Acidic, slightly moist soils that might be compacted or else clay soil with salts.

Feather grass, Mexican (*Nassella tenuissima*)
Indicates: Dry soils with a little salt and neutral to slightly alkaline pH.

Fennel (*Foeniculum vulgare*)
Indicates: Disturbed soils that are dry, low in nutrients and may contain salt.

Fiddleneck (*Amsinckia intermedia*)
Indicates: Dry and shallow soils that might have salt.

Filaree (*Erodium moschatum*)
Indicates: Soils that are dry, shallow with low to a little fertility.

Fireweed (*Chamerion angustifolium*)
Indicates: Dry, acidic and coarse or sandy soils that have low nutrients with little salt. A California native.

Fountain grass, crimson (*Pennisetum setaceum*)
Indicates: Dry soils with moderate fertility and neutral pH.

Groundsel (*Senecio* spp.)
Indicates: Dry, disturbed, shallow soils with low to moderate fertility.

Horehound (*Marrubium vulgare*)
Indicates: Dry and semi-fertile soils that might have salt.

Horsetail (*Equisetum* spp.)
Indicates: Moist soils that are low in salts with neutral to acidic pH. Many California natives.

Horseweed (*Erigeron canadensis*)
Indicates: Dry, disturbed, shallow soils that might be alkaline.

Jupiter's beard (*Centranthus ruber*)
Indicates: Dry, slightly acidic and low fertility soil that is probably silty.

Knapweed (*Acroptilon* spp.)
Indicates: Dry and disturbed soils with low to moderate fertility that might be clay, alkaline and have salt.

Knotweed (*Polygonum* spp.)
Indicates: Disturbed soils that might be moist and acidic. Some California natives.

Lamb's quarters (*Chenopodium album*)
Indicates: Might be a shady area with soil that is disturbed, shallow and has some organics.

Mexican evening primrose (*Oenothera speciosa*)
Indicates: Dry and shallow soils with occasional moisture, little to a few nutrients, and may indicate some salts.

Mugwort (*Artemisia douglasiana*)
Indicates: Wet to dry, low fertility and probably acidic soils. California native.

Mullein (*Verbascum* spp.)
Indicates: Dry to occasionally damp soils, disturbed, acidic with low fertility.

Mustard, black (*Brassica* spp.)
Indicates: Dry, disturbed, dense and shallow soils that might be alkaline and possess a little nitrogen and phosphorus.

Mustard, common or field (*Brassica rapa*)
Indicates: Deep, dry and disturbed soils that might be acidic and low in nutrients.

Nutgrass, nut sedge, Flatgrass (*Cyperus* spp.)
Indicates: Slightly moist and shallow soils with neutral to slightly acidic pH and possibly compaction. Some California natives.

Orchard grass (*Dactylis glomerata*)
Indicates: Moderately deep acidic soils that might have salt and be compacted.

Oxalis or Creeping wood sorrel (*Oxalis* spp.)
Indicates: Acidic, slightly fertile and moist soils that may be shallow and compacted.

Pennywort (*Hydrocotyle* spp.)
Indicates: Moist, fertile, and neutral pH soils.

Pigweed (*Amaranthus retroflexus*)
Indicates: Dry and disturbed soils with some nitrogen.

Plantain, common (*Plantago major*)
Indicates: Clay and slightly moist soils with low fertility and neutral to slightly acidic pH.

Poison hemlock (*Conium maculatum*)
Indicates: Slightly moist soils that are shallow with neutral to slightly acidic pH and some salts and nutrients.

Poison oak (*Toxicodendron diversilobum*)
Indicates: Dry shade and shallow soils that may have some salt. California native.

Prickly lettuce (*Lactuca serriola*)
Indicates: Dry and shallow soils with low fertility and some salt.

Purslane (*Portulaca oleracea*)
Indicates: Dry and disturbed soil with a little phosphorus and maybe salt.

Radish, wild (*Raphanus sativus*)
Indicates: Dry, disturbed, shallow soils, with low to some fertility that might be alkaline.

Ryegrass, (*Lolium* spp.)
Indicates: Dry and shallow soils with neutral pH and a little salt.

Scarlet pimpernel (*Lysimachia arvensis*)
Indicates: Some shade with a soil that might be slightly moist, with neutral pH, and some fertility.

Shepherd's purse (*Capsella bursa-pastoris*)
Indicates: Slightly moist, low nutrients and low salt soils.

Sowthistle (*Sonchus* spp.)
Indicates: Dry and shallow soils with neutral pH, little fertility and possibly some salt.

Sorrel, sheep (*Rumex acetosella*)
Indicates: Acidic, slightly moist and semi-shallow soils.

Spotted spurge (*Euphorbia maculate*)
Indicates: Dry and compacted soils that are low in salts with neutral to alkaline pH.

Stinging nettle (*Urtica* spp.)
Indicates: Lightly shaded and dry soils with neutral pH. Some California natives.

Thistle, bull (*Cirsium vulgare*)
Indicates: Shallow and salty soils with some fertility.

Thistle, Italian (*Carduus pycnocephalus*)
Indicates: Dry, shallow and slightly acidic soils with some nutrients and salts.

Thistle, prickly sow (*Sonchus asper*)
Indicates: Shallow soils with neutral to acidic pH, low fertility and salts.

Thistle, milk (*Silybum marianum*)
Indicates: Dry, shallow and/or clay soils, low to some fertility, and some salts.

Tree of heaven (*Ailanthus altissima*)
Indicates: Dry, shallow and slightly compacted soils that might have some fertility, salts and be slightly acidic.

Tree tobacco (*Nicotiana glauca*)
Indicates: Dry, disturbed, and shallow soils with a little salt.

Tumbleweed (*Salsola tragus*)
Indicates Dry and disturbed soils that might have salt.

Vetch (*Vicia* spp.)
Indicates: Dry shade and shallow and slightly acidic soils with low nutrients and nitrogen.

Yarrow, common (*Achillea millefolium*)
Indicates: Soils that might be slightly acidic and low in nutrients and potassium, with the possibility of salts. A California native.

11

Natural Pest Control

This chapter is for the land managers, gardeners and homeowners that not only want a pest-free landscape, but a chemical-free one as well—a landscape that is as good for them as for all the creatures that interact with it.

Many of the pests ravaging Southern California are listed below. A brief description is provided for each pest and includes the cultural, physical and biological remedies for its control.

Pest Free Landscapes

No landscape is pest-free, but some are more trouble-free than others. More likely than not, landscapes with fewer pests have some of the characteristics listed below:

- **Plant Compatibility**: One of the surest ways to reduce pests is to make sure than the plants chosen for the landscape are compatible with the environment and irrigation goals.

- **Good Horticultural Practices**: Irrigating correctly, pruning judiciously and at the right time, and fertilizing only when necessary will ensure plant health, which in turn reduces pest problems.

- **Cleanliness**: A common denominator for pest reduction is cleanliness. The places where pests live and breed have been eliminated. Old wood and leaf piles are removed; overgrown weedy areas are mowed and raked; and areas of storage are pulled out, swept and restacked.

- **Horticultural Diversity**: Having many different types of plants in a landscape ensures that if one plant gets infested, the entire landscape is not at risk. Horticultural diversity also reduces the likelihood of nutrient depletion and damage from climatic extremes.

- **Successional Diversity**: Succession is the process of one type of plant community transitioning to another type. Higher succession plants that have longer lives benefit from having shorter-lived, lower succession plants around them. See the explanation in the sidebar further on.

- **Know When to Quit**: Change is the only constant in living systems, and a landscape is a living system. It is always growing and evolving. What once was full sun may now be shade and soils originally alkaline may become acidic. Plants not compatible to evolving conditions will show signs of stress and pest infestation. At this point, just quit; instead remove the plant and replace it with one that is more compatible.

Successional Diversity

Successional trajectory is a theoretical model used to explain how landscapes recover from a disturbance, such as fire or flood. As an example: if a wildfire devours a forest, the forest would eventually return, but it would do so by a series of successions. The first plants to sprout after the fire would be the opportunists and pioneers, the low-succession annuals and biennials. The next succession would be the perennials, followed by scrub, shrub, mixed evergreen, and finally returning to forest.

In Southern California many of our most noxious pest problems occur on the longer- lived, higher-succession plants (food crops are an exception)—but the plants recommended to combat the pests, either by repelling them or attracting their predators, are lower-succession and shorter-lived. Simply put: Higher-succession plants are healthier when accompanied by lower-succession plants.

Lower-succession plants provide more benefits than just pest control and should be a part of every landscape. The reason they are not used more is because of their maintenance. These shorter-lived plants need more clean-ing, pruning, removing and replanting. However, the benefits of having these plants outweigh the change in (extra) maintenance. For a list of low-succes-sion, beneficial plants see the section on Companion Plants at the end of this chapter.

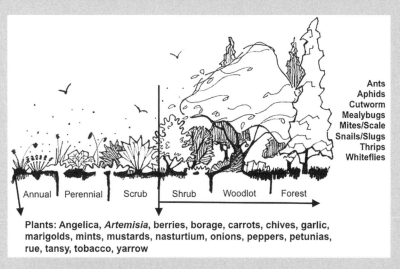

Ants
Aphids
Cutworm
Mealybugs
Mites/Scale
Snails/Slugs
Thrips
Whiteflies

Annual | Perennial | Scrub | Shrub | Woodlot | Forest

Plants: Angelica, *Artemisia*, berries, borage, carrots, chives, garlic, marigolds, mints, mustards, nasturtium, onions, peppers, petunias, rue, tansy, tobacco, yarrow

Using lower succession plants along with higher succession ones will help the landscape defend itself against pests. Lower succession plants attract beneficial insects, repel unwanted insects, and/or trap unwanted insects.

List of Pests

The list below has been separated into two parts: Animal pests and diseases/fungal pests. These lists been compiled over decades, including over 14 years at the Lyle Center for Regenerative Studies, Cal Poly Pomona. It also incorporates the work from the following publications:

■ *California Master Gardener Handbook*. Dennis R. Pittenger Editor. University of California: Agriculture and Natural Resources. Publication 3382. 2002.

■ *Pests of Landscape Trees and Shrubs: An Integrated Pest Management Guide*. Steve H. Dreistadt and Mary Louise Flint (Editor). University of California: Agriculture and Natural Resources. Publication 3359.

■ *Best Management Practices for Vegetation Management* (revised). Bell, Carl and Dean Lehman. Ellen Mackey, editor. Los Angeles Weed Management Area. 2015.

Animal Pests

Ants: Barriers such as sticky tape and roofing tar are good for keeping ants out of shrubs and trees. Lemon juice is a good deterrent when poured in the cracks ants occupy or travel in. Spearmint sprays (spearmint pureed, strained, and then added to 2 parts water) can be sprayed on the infected areas. Soap sprays (1 to 4 tablespoons per gallon of water) are used the same way as the spearmint sprays. Creating barriers around plants with diatomaceous earth works well. You can also plant catnip, pennyroyal, spearmint, southernwood or tansy to repel ants.

Aphids: Attracted to new growth and flowering parts, aphids prefer nutrient-rich leaves and humid environments. To deter them reduce the use of fertilizers and water, and prune to encourage airflow. Dislodge and disrupt aphids from foliage with a strong jet of water. The best homemade remedy is a soap spray (1 to 4 tablespoons per gallon of water). Other effective remedies include teas made from tobacco, onion, garlic, and shallots. Simply controlling ants can also reduce aphid population size. Plant angelica, chives, coriander, garlic, mustards, nasturtium, onions, petunias, southernwood, or spearmint as repellents. Encourage ladybug; their larvae devour aphids.

Black Widow Spiders: Preferring cool dark environments, these venomous spiders are found in wood and rubbish piles, underneath stilted structures, and inside irrigation boxes. Remove debris and clutter from around a structures. Never, ever, stick your hand into a dark place without sweeping the area first.

Cats: To deter cats from hunting, sleeping, and using the landscape as a restroom, make it as uncomfortable for them as possible. Lay thick, woody mulches over the area. Shield sandy play areas with palm fronds. Spread powders made of cayenne pepper and black pepper, or flour, mustard, cayenne, and chili powder over beds. Consider using orange and lemon peels; some gardeners claim that they are effective deterrents. You can also plant chives, garlic, or onions.

Cochineal: Cochineal is a biting sucking insect that attacks pancake cactus, cholla and some agaves. The best form of eradication is a strong jet of water to dislodge the colonies and then spraying the cacti with insecticidal soaps. Cochineal can also be brushed off with scrub brushes and toothbrushes. The bug is common in urban areas because of the incidental increase in moisture and nutrients.

Cockroaches: True urban dwellers, cockroaches can be found almost anywhere. They are decomposers and do not damage a landscape. To deter them keep the areas around a structure clean and free of piles of debris. Caulk cracks and protect small openings into a structure with a screen. Boric acid is a good repellent, and there are maze-like traps that work without chemicals.

Cutworms: Cutworms are the larvae of moths. They live at soil level and dine on vegetation within their reach. One of the quickest remedies is to till and turn over infected beds. Spread cornmeal across the area and they might die from indigestion. Lay mulches of eggshells, wood ashes, chicken manure, and oak leaves around new plants. Cut back wild grasses in fall in areas where moths lay their eggs. Plant tansy.

Deer: To the avid gardener deer are a serious nuisance. Keep them out with fences and barriers (an 8' fence is needed if see-through; 6' if solid). Protect individual plants with chicken wire. Plant deer-resistant plants, which tend to have small, brittle and resinous leaves. Deterrents include soap bars and hair hung in branches, and mixtures of garlic, capsaicin, peppermint, and rotting eggs spread around and over threatened plants. Dogs are sometimes good deterrents.

Dogs: Deter a dog through its nose. Spread dried and crushed red peppers or cayenne powder around the areas they like to visit. Plant thorny ground covers, such as bougainvillea and natal plum. Spread course mulches. Plant chives, garlic, or onions.

Fleas: The common remedies to this warm-season irritant are well-known: regularly vacuum carpets and wash/comb pets. Other strategies include using eucalyptus mulch around doghouses, kennels and houses; lay nylon stockings filled with the eucalyptus leaves throughout a house. Also, place a bowl full of soapy water under a light to attract and drown fleas at night. Attract or purchase beneficial nematodes for the landscape.

Grasshoppers: Although a seasonal problem, grasshoppers are voracious eaters and can do a lot of damage while they are around. They lay their eggs on undisturbed, weedy soil. Planting aggressive ground covers, protecting bare soil with coarse woody mulch, and/or disturbing the soil in early spring will help to reduce populations. Diatomaceous earth is an irritant and can also deter them. A spray made from the tea of hot peppers and small onions can be used as a deterrent too. *Nosema locustae*, a fungal disease that affects a grasshopper's digestive system, is another good organic remedy. Plant horehound.

Gophers: These herbivores eat the roots of many plants, including some succulents. Traps are the most effective remedy. You can shove castor beans and elderberry branches in their holes and runs. Burying ½" hardware cloth under beds is also effective. Be prepared to be diligent; every control method requires repeated efforts.

Hives: Not all hives of flying insects are bad. Yellow jackets and paper wasps are considered beneficial insects because they eat houseflies and other pests. Prevention is the best method of control; screen all openings and cracks with wire mesh 1/8 inch or smaller. Dislodge new hives with a jet of water. Call a professional if the hive is large. Mint oil sprayed around the places where wasps and hornets congregate is a good repellent.

Mealy Bugs: Much like the cochineal beetle, with whom it is often confused, mealy bugs are biting, sucking insects. These cottony masses thrive in warm, humid environments. Dry the area and prune to improve air circulation. Use a strong jet of water to dislodge mealy bugs. Swipe a thin cloth dampened with rubbing alcohol to kill them. A mixture of dish soap and water is an effective deterrent, too, as is kerosene and water (both mixtures are 1 to 4 tablespoons per gallon of water). Also control the ants that help distribute them.

Mites: These tiny bugs are attracted to dusty environments and water-stressed plants. Make sure that the affected plant is not over or under watered. Use a strong jet of water to dislodge the insects and clean the foliage. Soap sprays and neem oil are effective controls. So is capsaicin and water (1 to 4 tablespoons per gallon of water). Mites are not true insects and insecticides do not work well against them; miticides are available if the problem is severe.

Moles: These diggers tend to do more damage in heavily watered landscapes. Let the soil dry. Traps are the surest remedy. Burying ½" hardware cloth under beds is also effective. You could try cramming a variety of items in the outlets and runs, including garlic, human hair, moth crystals, thorny stems, elderberry leaves and stems, caster oil or seeds, rotten eggs, and hot peppers. Visit the area daily and keep shoving the repellents back in their holes. Plant daffodils and castorbean.

Mosquitos: A California Friendly landscape would not provide the opportunity for mosquitos. Although only a tiny amount of water is needed to breed mosquitos, the water needs to be stagnant for at least 7 days; modern irrigation would rarely enable this type of water accumulation. But the reality is not everyone irrigates with conservation and mosquitos in mind. Citronella is good repellent. Rosemary and catnip can be rubbed directly on clothes, or made into a tea and sprayed on clothes and skin. If collecting water in an open system, then use *Bacillus thuringiensis israelensis* (Bt), available at any hardware store. Plant ageratum, basil, castorbean, catnip, marigold, or rosemary. For a more thorough discussion see the chapter on Rainwater Capture.

Pine Beetles: Pine beetles attack weak and water-stressed trees and are a serious problem in the Southern California foothills. Chemical controls are extreme and expensive. It is better to remove infested trees in winter (when the beetles are less active), prune damaged branches as you spot them, increase distance between trees, and deeply water trees in the long, dry summer months.

Rabbits: Rabbits are common in urban developments bordering natural areas. Dogs and cats can be deterrents. Laying coarse mulches, such as recently chipped trees, eggshells, and bramble, around new and vulnerable plantings helps. Mulches of pepper sauce, daffodil bulbs, iris rhizomes, catnip, and spearmint may work as well. Blood meal, bone meal and wood ashes are known deterrents. Mothballs can deter them, but should not be used around children. Plant anything in the onion family, such as chives, garlic, or onions. However, fencing is the surest way to protect particular plants or areas within a landscape from rabbits.

Scale: Scale are related to mites and, like these insects, thrive in dusty, humid environments. Make sure that the plant is not over or under watered. Use a strong jet of water to dislodge the insects and clean the foliage. Maintain healthy plants. Scale are protected by a shell; to remove scrape off or wipe off bugs with a cloth dipped in alcohol or turpentine. Horticultural oil and dormant sprays, such as neem oil, will suffocate them and are effective in spring and summer. Control the ants that help distribute them.

Skunks: Although feared by humans, skunks are good for a garden. They have a diverse appetite and eat fallen fruit, bugs, beetles and mice, all of which can be pests. If a nuisance, get rid of their homes by cleaning or removing woodpiles, cleaning drainage pipes, covering all openings into a structure, (such as crawl spaces) and rousting other small hiding spots. Make sure the lids of trash cans are on tight.

Snails and Slugs: Snails and slugs should not be a problem in a California Friendly landscape since they need consistent moisture to flourish. It stands to reason that the most effective remedy is letting the landscape dry. Build a trap by stacking moist wood and in the afternoon when they are hiding they can easily be picked out. Empty beer cans are a good trap too. The next best control is to physically remove them by hand at night. Eliminate high grasses, weeds, piles of debris and other places where they hide and breed. Copper strips provide a good barrier, especially around raised beds and containers, but may only be effective for a short period. Protect the base of plants with anything coarse, such as used sandpaper, berry brambles, oak leaves, diatomaceous earth, or wood ashes. A tea made from wormwood can also deter them. Sprinkling salt will desiccate them. Plant prostrate juniper, rosemary and wormwood to repel; chervil and sorrel to trap.

Spider Mites: Attracted to dry, dusty environments, this tiny biting mite creates a colony of webbing on the underside of leaves. Spider mites spread easily if plants are grown too close together. Remove or prune plants to create more open, breezy spaces. Make sure that the plant is not over or under watered. Use a strong jet of water to dislodge the insects and clean the foliage. The presence of this bug may indicate an oversupply nutrients; so do not fertilize again until there are signs of deficiencies. Apply dormant spray or horticultural oil in spring. Spray a mixture of ground limestone and dish soap. If organic methods do not work, then apply a miticide. Plant chives, garlic, and onions.

Thrips: Though widely distributed, thrips are a pest that prefers flowers and fruit. Mowing wild weeds helps enormously. The insects can be blown off with a jet of water or manually scraped off. A mixture of canola oil and water is a good repellent (1 to 2 teaspoons of canola mixed with 1 gallon of water); or use tobacco tea, oil, and water; or a paste of 1 part yeast, 1 part sugar mixed with water and smeared on flower buds. Plant alyssum, clover, coriander, cosmos, dill, mustard and yarrow to attract green lacewings, a predator of thrips.

Whiteflies: These insects are common in humid environments with poor air circulation. Prune plants to open up the foliage and dry the area. Sticky tape will ensnarl them and jets of water will dislodge them, both of which are the quickest controls. Insecticidal soaps are an effective control, as are teas and dusts made from tobacco. Ladybugs eat whiteflies. Plant marigold and tree tobacco as deterrents; nasturtium as a trap.

Disease and Fungal Pests

Black Spot: This is a disease that causes black spots and yellow margins on leaves. Proper irrigation is key: avoid watering the foliage; let the soil dry between watering; and never irrigate during periods of high humidity. Prune the plants to increase air circulation. Pull back mulch to increase soil temperature. Throw away the diseased plant parts. A spray of 6 tablespoons of vinegar to 1 gallon of water may work, but use cautiously as the vinegar can harm some plants (test first). Another good spray is 1 teaspoon of baking soda per 1 quart of water, plus a few drops of dish soap.

Blight: The term blight refers to a number of diseases, most of which prefer moist, humid, and hot environments. Cut back on watering and prune to allow sun to strike the soil. Not much can be done for infected plants except removing the infected parts. However, deterring the insects that spread the disease, such as aphids, can slow its spread. If caught early, try a spray of 2 tablespoons of bleach and 2 tablespoons of baby shampoo in 1 gallon of water.

Powdery Mildew: This fungus covers blossoms and leaves with a thin layer of chalky growth. It prefers shade. Pruning helps a lot; it increases sunlight, improves air circulation, and removes infected parts. Counter to many of the other funguses, powdery mildew does not like to be wet; wash blooms and leaves at first sign of the disease. Powdery mildew may indicate over fertilization so do not fertilize again unless the landscape shows signs of deficiency. Good fungal sprays are 1 tablespoon of baking soda and 1 to 2 teaspoons of canola oil mixed with 1 gallon of water, or 3 tablespoons of vinegar to 1 gallon of water.

Root Rot: Root rot is caused by any number of funguses that kill the plant at or below its base. Improve soil drainage by working amendments, such as mulch and compost, into the soil. Dramatically cut back on watering. Plant rot-resistant varieties.

Rust: This fungal disease appears as an orange spotted mass that typically inhabits the underside of leaves. It spreads by water and wind. Switching from overhead irrigation to low-flow can help a lot. Remove contaminated vegetation from property. Keep areas around plants clean of debris during the wet months. Prune to increase sunlight and air circulation. If none of these measures work, replant with more rust-resistant varieties.

Sooty Mold: This fungus creates a thin, sticky black and gray film that coats leaves. It is as ugly as it is damaging. Sooty mold thrives on the honeydew of bugs and is usually a sign of other pests. It can also be a sign of high humidity and poor air circulation. First, control the bugs that are secreting the honeydew, which are typically aphids, mealy bugs, scale and whiteflies. A firm jet of water will reduce all populations. Prune the area to increase sunlight and wind. Keep the area dry.

Companion Plants

A companion plant is one that improves the health of the plants growing around it. Companion plants can be used to attract pollinators, control pests, enrich soil, or improve the flavor of certain crops. For pest control there are three general categories of companion plants: plants that attract a pest's predator, plants that repel pests, and plants that trap pests. The use of companion plants will not solve pest problems alone, but they are an effective addition to the other strategies offered in this chapter.

Nasturtium has been planted between this row of fruit trees to help trap aphids. Marigold has been planted to discourage nematodes and whiteflies. Orange Homegrown Community Farm, Orange.

Plants that Attract

The purpose of these plants is to attract the insects that will eat the pests you want to eliminate. They do it by providing food and water or breeding and resting opportunities for them. Plants that attract beneficial insects include alyssum, angelica, aster, basil, black-eyed Susan, blanket flowers, buckwheat, coreopsis, coriander, cosmos, dill, fennel, feverfew, mustard, sage, tansy, tidy tips, and yarrow.

Plants that Repel

These are the plants that some pests actively dislike and try to avoid. They include angelica, basil, chive, clover, eucalyptus, garlic, leek, marigold, mint, mustard, onion, petunia, rosemary, southernwood and tobacco.

Plants that Trap

The goal of these plants is to attract unwanted pests, pulling them away from favored plants. Though they are sacrificial, they still need attention—the pests they attract will become a problem if not handled. Pruning or removing the infested vegetation and then replanting is necessary. Some of the plants that attract unwanted pests include basil, chervil, clover, datura, fennel, lamb's quarter, marigold, nasturtium, pelargonium, sorrel, sunflower and wild radish.

There are three strategies to help these plants have a bigger impact. First, ensure that something is in bloom most of the year; spring, summer and fall flowers are all needed. Second, pick at least three plants for each season, meaning that at a minimum a landscape will have 9 types of companion plants. Third, plant the same plant in groups of twos and threes: the greater the mass, the greater its effect.

PART V

Stormwater

12

Stormwater: Infiltrating, Screening and Cleaning Runoff

Water is essential for life, and stormwater management is important because it protects this essential resource. The EPA has said that stormwater runoff is the largest source of urban water pollution and a major source of pollution for all waterbodies in the U.S. In Southern California stormwater runoff creates 80% of all ocean pollution. California is aware of the impact of stormwater runoff and has taken action.

Whether through building codes, voluntary certification, or simple advocacy, California has built tens of thousands of small-scale stormwater management systems. All these systems need maintenance to properly perform. But, because up to 70% of urban areas are under impervious cover and up to 50% of all rainfall turns into runoff, managing stormwater systems requires both skill and time.

Managing stormwater involves slowing, infiltrating, and screening and cleaning runoff. This chapter is focused on the last three aspects of the process. Slowing runoff and managing surfaces, which are also a vital parts of stormwater management, are covered in the following chapter. At the end of this chapter is a bulleted checklist for action.

Just Before the Start of the Rains

Handling stormwater in Southern California means that a majority of the maintenance occurs in mid to late fall, just before the first rains. These annual tasks include:

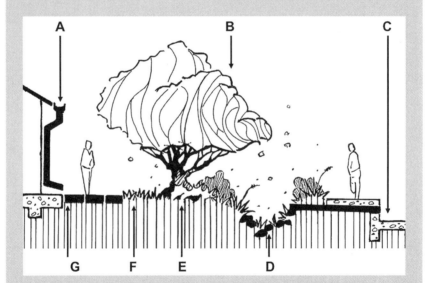

A. Clean gutters, filters and screens.

B. Protect infrastructure, such as structures and utility lines, from vegetation.

C. Sweep and clean curbs and culverts.

D. Remove sediment from infiltration areas.

E. Mulch exposed soil.

F. Aerate compacted soils.

G. Sweep or vacuum impermeable surfaces.

Infiltrating Runoff

An infiltration basin, often called a rain garden, is an area designed to capture runoff and allow the water to sit and soak. There are two types of infiltration: above-ground and below-ground. Above-ground infiltration devices are preferred over below-ground. Above-ground devices are quickly and inexpensively constructed, and are also easily monitored, altered, and maintained. Below-ground devices are usually used only when space is limited.

Water that runs will move things. Leaves, litter and toxic residues all end up in infiltration basins. Maintenance is essential to a well functioning and healthy system.

Above Ground Infiltration

Dry Stack Walls: Dry stack walls are a quick and efficient way to stop runoff on low to medium steep slopes. They are usually short walls running mostly perpendicular to a slope or water path. Two types of problems occur and two types of maintenance are required. First, dirt and debris will collect on the wall's upslope side, reducing its water holding and slowing capacity, while increasing pressure on the structure. Remove this accumulation every 2 to 4 years. Second, the downward side of the wall will erode, eventually undermining it. Every 2 to 3 years pull the soil back up to the wall and either plant to stabilize or compact it.

Infiltration Basins/Seasonal Ponds: Landscaped depressions are anything that allows water to sit and slowly infiltrate. Infiltration areas require vegetation management, such as pruning and thinning as well as the removal of sediment. Ideally, dirt, debris and sludge should be removed from a basin when it loses 10% of its capacity, which occurs approximately every 2 to 6 years depending on use. Avoid trampling and compacting the soil when cleaning the basin; pick specific paths and lay down boards to protect soils. For vegetation management, see the sidebar later in the chapter.

The rocky depression pictured is plumbed to capture the roof water and regularly fills with debris, leaves and weeds. Like all depressions, this infiltration area needs a thorough cleaning every other year.

Micro Basins: Micro basins are simply small depressions dug into a landscape. They are quick to construct and effective on flat to medium steep slopes. Over time these basins will fill with dirt and debris, so re-grading will be necessary every 2 to 4 years.

Rain Gardens: Rain gardens are used when space is tight and runoff great. They might employ both above- and below-ground devices, such as an infiltration basin and dry well. They can also be as simple as a raised planter. The above ground areas fill rapidly with dirt, debris and plants and will need cleaning every other year. If runoff is run through aggregate with only cursory screening, then the small rock may have to be pulled up and washed every 5 years. Because of the rich, porous soil, plants thrive in rain gardens. Consequently they will need regular maintenance. Vegetation Management is covered in detail later in this chapter.

Swales: Swales are built to move runoff through a landscape. Swales are earthen, or have earthen bottoms, and allow for infiltration. A grass and rock lined swale can stop up to 85% of the runoff from a small to medium rain event. Dirt and debris fill these sinuous depressions, and re-grading will be needed every 3 to 5 years. Soil slumps are not uncommon occurrences in swales, and rebuilding a swale's wall may be necessary during the rainy season. Weeds are a constant problem; their management is covered in the Weed Control chapter.

A colony of crabgrass has taken root in this rocky swale. If not removed, the crabgrass might affect the flow of water and cause unwanted pooling elsewhere.

Vegetation Management

Vegetation is excellent at stopping rain from becoming runoff. Turf is good, but trees and shrubs are even better. As opposed to lawns, between to 30% to 50% more rain is captured in landscapes planted with trees, shrubs and ground covers. Unfortunately, vegetation has its own set of problems. Plants can change a soil's grade and become a nuisance to urban infrastructure. Use the tips below to effectively manage vegetation in infiltration areas.

Fertilizing: Because everything gravitates toward a depression, infiltration areas get plenty of nutrients and rarely need fertilization. Don't apply fertilizer unless you see signs of nutrient deficiency. If fertilization is needed, follow these guides to reduce leaching: Never fertilize before or during the rainy season; use easily digestible fertilizers, such as fish emulsion; and decrease the amount applied by half to two-thirds, but fertilize more frequently.

Pesticides: Because they are moister areas than the rest of the landscape, infiltration areas tend to attract weeds, insects, and fungus. However using pesticides and herbicides to control these problems undermines the whole purpose of the basin—which is improving the quality of our water. Therefore pesticides and herbicides should always be avoided; use the principles of Integrated Pest Management (IPM) instead. Refer to the chapter on Weed Control for alternatives to harmful herbicides.

Pruning: Plants grow vigorously in infiltration areas because they have moist and rich soil. Pruning is necessary to protect people, infrastructure, and to ensure good air circulation, which will reduce many pests. Whether dividing or thinning, try to avoid pruning just before or during the rainy season. Refer to the Plant chapters for specific pruning recommendations.

Renewal: Replant dead, dying and diseased vegetation with evergreen plants, not deciduous ones. A deciduous tree can catch up to 760 gallons of rainwater a year, a mature evergreen up to 4,000 gallons. Deciduous trees not only intercept less rain, they also litter profusely. Some can drop 400 pounds of leaf litter a year. Deciduous vegetation is not recommended near impervious surfaces that lead to storm drains, such as parking lots and streets.

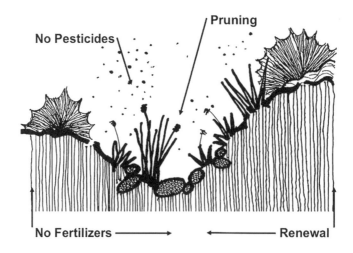

Below-Ground Infiltration

Below-ground infiltration devices are used where space is limited. These devices are expensive to construct and demand a greater amount of attention. Because debris and sediment will eventually fill or clog these devices, screening and cleaning the incoming water is essential to system longevity.

Dry/Infiltration Wells: A dry well is a large pit lined with filter fabric and filled with a variety of porous objects. See the illustration below for specific maintenance tasks.

A.* Make sure leaf guards are secure and in working condition.

B. Test the first-rain diversion device to make sure it is operational.

C. Clean the ¼" screen within the downspout once a month during the rainy season.

D.* Check or install a flap gate on the overflow pipe if mosquitos or vermin are a problem.

E. Remove sediment from the below-ground canister every year to every third year, depending on use and number of screens

F. Lift up, wash, and reset the entire system if infiltration falls to unacceptable levels. If new aggregate is needed, then use rounded drain rock 1" to 1.5" in diameter.

G.* Make sure that the inspection port has no opening so that insects cannot enter the chamber below

---

*Note: Mosquitoes will fly surprisingly long distances down pipes to reach water. It is critical, especially for below ground cisterns, that pipes and vents be screened if they are open to the atmosphere and one-way valves or flaps are installed on overflow pipes. ■

French Drains/Infiltration Trenches/Recharge Trenches: These three types of infiltration drains are long, fabric-lined trenches filled with rounded aggregate and gravel. They are used to sink water and transport it, typically away from a structure. Unfortunately, and due to dirty run-off, these devices can the fail within 5 years. Debris and grit will fill the aggregate's void space and/or clog the fabric's pores. System longevity depends on slowing the water and properly screening it.

Infiltration and Surfacing Water

Once underground, water will move in any direction that provides the least resistance, and sometimes that direction can lead back to the surface. Unfortunately surfacing water can have some unfortunate consequences. It can speed the decay of walkways and roadways, it can cause soil to move, and it can increase rates of erosion. Surfacing water needs to be identified and its risks known. Below are some of the signs and risks of surfacing water.

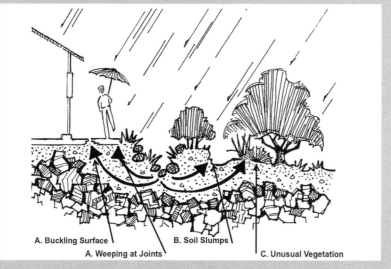

A. Buckling Surface
A. Weeping at Joints
B. Soil Slumps
C. Unusual Vegetation

A. Seepage from underneath concrete or asphalt, such as sidewalks and roadways, will cause the surface to crack and will widen those cracks. It will also weaken the bonds in asphalt and speed its decay. If infiltration leads to seepage in concrete or asphalt, then steps should be taken to stop or reduce it.

B. Soil moves with water and sometimes that movement is harmful. Soil slumps may occur around the edges of infiltration basins, micro basins and swales. The movement and slumps can redirect water and cause further problems. If movement occurs, rebuild the slope and either use plants or rocks to hold it in place.

C. The outcropping of certain weeds can indicate surfacing water. Plants such as curly dock, moss, nutgrass, and reeds will naturally colonize areas of seepage. Problems with these areas include soil movement and a breeding ground for pests, such as mosquitos and fungus. If soil movement or pests persist, then reduce or stop infiltration.

Screening Runoff

Directing runoff through a device to remove debris is essential to stormwater management—it is vital in protecting the state's waterbodies. Of all the stormwater strategies, screening devices are the most common and require the most maintenance.

Core Maintenance Tasks

Although there are many different screening devices, they all share some core maintenance tasks:

- Clean all screening devices before the start of the rain in mid to late fall. They should also be checked again after any rain event of a 1" or more.

- Maintain good accessibility. Maintenance may be required frequently and good accessibility will make the job quick and easy, especially in areas with a lot of leaf litter.

- Clean the overflow outlet at least once a year. At some point all screening devices will become overwhelmed and if the runoff is not quickly ushered away, then erosion and infrastructural problems will follow.

Catch Basins: Clean all catch basins and sediment traps before the start of the rains. These devices may need additional cleaning throughout the wet season, especially in areas with a lot of leaf litter.

Once a year the grate to this catch basin should be lifted and the debris and sediment scooped out.

Curb Cuts: Cutting into curbs and culverts allows runoff to flow into the landscape. Making sure that runoff can flow freely through these inlets is essential before the start of the rains in late fall. Both debris and excess vegetation will have to be removed.

Stormwater management will only work with a long-term commitment to maintenance. The grasses blocking the curb cut pictured above will cause water to pool on the asphalt, which speeds the surface's decay and creates a public hazard.

Fiber Rolls: Fiber rolls are straw, rice hulls or coconut waste bound by strong plastic mesh. They are used around storm drains and on slopes. Fiber rolls degrade quickly and need to be removed before they become a litter problem; their life span is normally no more than two years.

Filter Cloth: Typically made from nylon, these fabrics are not only used to filter solids out of runoff, but also particles out of the air. They are a common feature on construction sites, where fabric may surround a property and/or has been laid over storm drains. Filter cloth has a limited life and should be removed after two years.

Gabions: Gabions, which are large or small walls made from rock bound by a wire cage, are used to protect storm drains, act as check dams, or simply put in front of the flow of runoff to slow and screen the water. Every 2 to 4 years gabions will need to be cleaned by a power-washer to remove accumulated debris and dirt.

Mulch: Mulches can slow runoff, increase infiltration and filter out debris. For greater detail on mulches, refer to the next chapter.

Sediment Pond/Trap: A sediment pond is a widening in a channel that allows the water to slow enough to drop its heavier particles. These areas can be permeable or not, vegetated or not. Every 2 to 5 years, depending on use, the sediment from these areas will have to be removed.

Trench Drain Grates: Typically used at the end of driveways, trench drains stop sheeting water from going into the street or storm drain system. Trench drains need to be cleaned before the rains every year. Grates will weaken in high traffic areas and will need replacing if broken.

Cleaning Runoff

Constructed wetlands are built on large commercial and institutional properties to handle the site's polluted runoff. They employ bacteria, bugs, fungus and plants to clean the water. Chromium, fertilizers, hydrocarbons, iron, lead, mercury, oil, pathogens, pesticides and solvents are either pulled from the water, or transformed into less harmful substances. Professionals generally maintain constructed wetlands and are knowledgeable in handling water and managing waste.

There are 3 primary tasks for maintaining constructed wetlands: removing toxins, removing sediment, and corralling plants.

Removing Toxins: While many of the toxins may have been removed from the runoff, they are still present in the environment, either locked in soils and/or plant tissue. These harmful pollutants, mainly metals, still need to be disposed of in a place where they will not be able to harm humans or other organisms. If heavy metals are detected in the plant tissue or sediment, the wetland's debris must be hauled to a local hazardous waste facility.

Removing Sediment: Ideally, dirt, debris and sludge should be removed from a constructed wetland when it loses 10% of its capacity (approximately every 2 to 6 years). Avoid trampling and compacting the soil when cleaning the basin. If the sediment contains metals, such as lead or mercury, it should be hauled to a hazardous waste facility.

Corralling Plants: The plants able to thrive in constructed wetlands are special. They are fast breathers, heavy feeders, and rapid growers. Cattail, reeds, sedges and willow dominate these environments and all will overrun a wetland if not corralled. Dividing, pruning, removing, thinning, and replanting are ongoing tasks, and maintenance should be expected no less than twice a year.

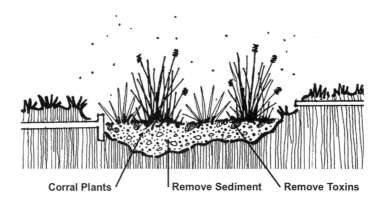

Corral Plants   **Remove Sediment**   **Remove Toxins**

A Stormwater Checklist

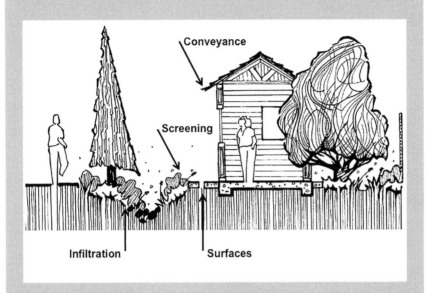

Conveyance Systems: Gutters, Culverts and Curbs

■ Remove debris and leaves from storm drain transport systems before rain. Poorly maintained storm drain systems are the leading cause of erosion in urban areas.

■ Remove the build up of debris and sludge from swales. Soil slumps are not uncommon in swales and rebuilding may be necessary during the rainy season.

■ Always guide runoff away from bare dirt areas, such as garden paths, because it causes rutting and gullies.

Screening Systems

■ Clean all catch basins and sediment traps before the start of the rains. These devices may need additional cleaning throughout the wet season, especially in areas with a lot of leaf litter.

■ Repair or replace leaf guards in gutters and downspouts.

■ Fix or replace stormwater drain grates.

■ Clean gabions with high-pressure water.

■ Remove debris and sediment from behind any device running perpendicular to a slope, such as check dams and fiber rolls.

■ Check screening systems after any rain event of 1" or more.

Surfaces

■ Every year vigorously sweep or vacuum pervious surfaces. Hosing a surface does not always improve its permeability.

■ Mulch planted areas to buffer soil from rain. Ideally, the mulch will come from material generated onsite.

■ Aerate landscaped areas that are compacted or trampled; then cover in 1" to 2" of mulch.

■ Keep planted areas below paved or semi-permeable surfaces. Refer to the section on grading a California Friendly landscape in the next chapter.

Infiltration Area

■ Remove sediment and leafy debris from infiltration basins when 10% of the capacity has been reduced.

■ Divide, prune, thin, and/or remove overgrown plants at least once a year.

■ Dig up and clean underground infiltration devices every 5 to 10 years, depending on use and the cleanliness of the water flowing through it.

13

Managing Surfaces and Slowing Runoff

All surfaces require maintenance. Below are the maintenance requirements for the surfaces most commonly used in stormwater management; the land covers that slow runoff and increase infiltration.

This chapter deals with walking surfaces, mulches, overcoming compacted soils and maintaining the grade of a California Friendly landscape.

A California Friendly Landscape actively manages its surfaces, whether they be mulch, gravel, river rock, or DG. This picture illustrates good surface management. LADWP's headquarters, Los Angeles.

Walking/Driving Surfaces

Brick/Pavers: Vigorously sweep or vacuum pervious surfaces at least once a year, monthly is better. Do not hose or power-wash, as both will eventually create an impermeable layer of ultra-fine debris. Letting weeds grow and then flaming them will increase permeability. Brick or pavers not set in concrete will move, drop and lift, and every 4 to 7 years they will need to be removed, the area re-graded, and everything reset.

No permeable surface is without maintenance. Bricks and pavers need sweeping or vacuuming, weeding, and resetting. Huntington Beach.

Decking: Decks are great for stormwater management. They slow water, prevent the soil beneath from becoming compacted, and are made from renewable materials. Decks should be budgeted for replacement every 10-15 years, depending on climate, exposure, maintenance and use. If stained, wood will need to be repainted every 3 to 5 years.

Decomposed Granite (DG): As a walking surface (not mulch), DG will need maintenance at least once a year. DG moves and needs annual corralling and re-grading. DG also becomes muddy looking over time. When it does so scrape off just enough DG to get back to the original material and color. Moist, damp and/or shady areas attract molds, mosses and grime and will require more frequent scraping. Hauling in new DG for replenishment will be needed every 3 to 5 years, and more frequently on any type of slope. If weeds are a problem, scrap, use a push broom or flame every 4 weeks, or before the weed sets seed. Avoid using any chemical on DG, including herbicides, because it can discolor the surface.

DG can get muddy looking over time. Scrap off and haul away just enough DG to get back to original material. Eventually, new material will have to be hauled in.

Dirt: Dirt is a great mulch, but a terrible weed suppressant. It can hold moisture, cool roots and provide nutrients. The smoother the dirt, the faster water runs, so grading soil so that it has slight rises and falls will slow runoff, allowing for greater rates of infiltration. If possible, leave a layer of natural debris on top of the soil to slow evaporation and protect it from wind erosion. Avoid excessive hoeing; it will degrade the soil.

This dirt thoroughfare allows easy access, is low maintenance, and the pine needles help suppress weeds. California State University, Fullerton.

Flat Stone: Broken concrete pavers and natural or recycled stone set in dirt or sand are common materials for pathways and patios. The gaps between stones need regular weeding and edging, and sometimes irrigating. Preemergent herbicides work well to reduce frequency of weeding. The soil between the gaps should be kept an inch below the surface of the stone to increase water-holding capacity and protect the plants from trampling. Stone not set in concrete will move and lift, and every 4 to 7 years the stone will need to be removed, the area re-graded, and the stones reset. Always protect fingers and wear gloves when working in the gaps.

Inorganic Mulches: Covered later.

Organic Mulches: Covered later.

Porous Asphalt / Concrete: Porous surfaces can lose 75% efficiency in 5 years through the natural accumulation of dust and fine debris. Cleaning is essential; monthly is best. Vacuuming is the most effective way of removing fine grit and debris. Next best is sweeping and blowing. Avoid high-pressure hoses because the spray will loosen the bonds and pry apart the aggregate, degrading the surface. Be sure to identify areas that contribute debris to the surface and try to reduce their impact. Avoid using fine mulches, select trees with little leaf drop, and, if there are surrounding areas with bare earth, plant or seed to cover them.

Both the porous concrete and pavers will need periodic vacuuming or sweeping to maintain efficiency.

Turf Blocks: Though beautiful and highly permeable, turf blocks require frequent maintenance. If not driven or walked on, the area will need regular mowing. Weeds are usually abundant and pulling or scraping are the most successful strategies to deal with them. The plants and soil will eventually grow over the blocks and scraping off the excess and reseeding may be needed every 5 years.

Mulches

Mulches provide incredible benefits—they slow evaporation, suppress weeds, enrich the soil, reduce topsoil loss, increase rainwater infiltration, regulate soil temperature, and/or make an area look more attractive. But they can cause problems, too.

Mulches are can disguise irrigation problems. They can alter the chemistry of soil. They can not only shorten some plants' lives, but also favor non-native weeds. And some types of mulches can increase the ignitability of a landscape and become a liability in fire country.

Mulches can be used to great effect, but in order to do so requires understanding the differences between mulches and to align that understanding with a landscape's needs. Mulch recommendations are made in the Plant chapters for many California Friendly plants. Below are the most common mulches, their characteristics, and their best uses.

Mulches are grouped between organic and inorganic.

Inorganic Mulches

Inorganic mulches have grown in popularity. In some cases they are used for purely aesthetic reasons, in other cases they are used to suppress weeds and enhance plant health. They are an ideal mulch for many durable plants, such as California native shrub plants and cacti. Inorganic mulches require maintenance, although it is much lower than other land cover options.

Crushed Aggregate: Crushed aggregate and gravel are inexpensive and ideal for many types of Mediterranean landscapes. Aggregate moves and will eventually migrate out of its area. Replenishment of aggregate will be needed every 3 to 5 years. If replenishing, make sure that the aggregate has been washed of fine dust before laying over the soil; the dust will create a thin impermeable layer just below the rock. Gravel will work its way into a soil and landscape fabric is needed for separation. There is no way to keep weeds out and if not pulling or scraping, then flaming will be needed. At least twice a year blow the material to remove debris.

Chipped granite mulch has some advantages over DG. It does not get compacted like DG. It is not as compatible to weeds. And many people believe it looks better. It is also, however, more expensive than DG. Newport Beach City Hall.

Decomposed Granite (DG): DG is a good mulch for desert, Mediterranean and many California native plants. Unfortunately, non-compacted and non-stabilized DG is a perfect medium for many weeds. While weeds may be plentiful in this medium, they are also easy to control. Nearly every technique for eradication is effective. See the Weed chapter for greater detail.

Fiber rolls are protecting the sidewalk from the DG mulch. The DG should be removed. Not only does it have a tendency to travel on slopes, but it is easy to compact and quickly produces runoff. DG is ill advised on slopes.

Plastic Sheeting: Plastic sheets are laid over soil to reduce evaporation, increase soil temperatures, and suppress, if not kill weeds. The plastic, generally polyethylene, breaks down rapidly and can pollute the soil as it does so. Plastic sheeting should be pulled from the soil within 6 months. If long-term weed suppression is needed, then less toxic, more natural materials, such as cardboard and weed fabric are recommended.

River Rock: Though beautiful in appearance, ideal for Mediterranean plants, and a good solution for shady and windy areas, river rock has several disadvantages. For one thing, it is one of the most expensive mulches. It is also a difficult mulch to weed. Weeds will eventually root in the debris that has settled on the landscape fabric, and reaching in and around rocks to remove them makes weeding a time-consuming task. Flaming is an option if the rock is more than 6" deep and there is no leafy debris. Note, the smaller the river rock, the easier it is to weed. At least twice a year vacuum or blow the rock to remove debris.

River rock has many uses. The stone can help enable infiltration, become a walking surface, and provide strong aesthetic elements. Cal Poly Pomona.

Organic Mulches

Almost any organic residue can be used as mulch, but not all mulches are the same or have the same effect on a landscape. Listed below are the mulches most commonly used in Southern California, along with their best uses, ability to suppress weeds, and amounts of available nutrients.

Organic mulches come from milling operations (shavings and saw-dust are an example), repurposed wood, such as pallets and construction debris, agricultural byproducts, such as manures and bedding, greenwaste collection, such as compost and recently chipped trees, or straight from the property, such as compost made from kitchen scraps and leaves. The pH of organic mulches ranges from neutral to slightly acidic, with coffee grounds, humus and peat moss being absolutely acidic. Manures will contain salt and might be alkaline.

Bark: Bark is available in three sizes. Fine bark is a good walking surface and the fastest to decompose. Large bark is good for holding soil in windy, exposed areas. All bark will initially rob the soil of nitrogen. When bark is completely decomposed it will have contributed small amounts of nitrogen, phosphorus and potassium. Because of its expense, bark is not an ideal weed suppressant on large properties.

Burlap Sacks: Heavy and organic, burlap sacks are good at suppressing weeds and holding topsoil. These bags are cut open, laid on the soil, and sometimes held down with other mulches. If kept moist, burlap is quick to decompose, at which point it is either worked into the soil or pulled up and composted elsewhere. The sacks have little nutrients. Burlap can be purchased at craft stores. The sacks might also be available at coffee shops.

Cardboard / Newspaper: These materials are generally used to help smother a landscape. They are laid on top of soil or plants and then buried with a layer of mulch 4" or thicker. This is an effective strategy for weed suppression. The nutrient levels of cardboard and newspaper are low but when combined with mulch the soil will be become much richer once the material has decomposed.

Deterring versus Nourishing Mulches

For purposes of simplicity, organic mulches can be divided between deterring and nourishing. Deterring mulches are used to suppress weeds and are woody, high in carbon, and made from materials that are slow to decompose such as eucalyptus and camphor. Deterring mulches will initially rob the soil of nitrogen and are slow to give it back. Nourishing mulches are used to support plant health and growth. They are in a further state of decomposition and contain all kinds of microorganisms and nutrients.

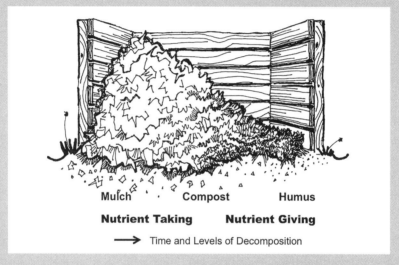

Deterring mulches are used as weed suppression on landscapes with low nutrient needs. They are commonly used around native, Mediterranean and succulent plants. Nourishing mulches are excellent for food crops, acid-loving tropical and temperate plants, and landscapes where plant productivity is either desired or required.

A 4" layer of woody course mulch will suppress weeds. It is too thick to support seed germination and it will initially rob the soil of nitrogen.

Colored Mulch: More expensive and decorative, colored mulches are made from woody debris and offer all the same benefits as non-colored. Color is provided by water-based dyes such as iron oxide and carbon black. Current research says that these dyes do not increase health risks to plants, soil organisms, pets or humans.

Compost: Compost is simply organic material that has decomposed. Ideally, the compost was brought to a temperature that kills weed seeds and pathogens. Compost does not rob nutrients from the soil, but typically is not decomposed enough to supply abundant nutrients immediately. The amount of nutrients in compost varies according the materials that created it. Compost is great for nourishing landscapes, but it is poor at weed suppression.

Cocoa Hulls: Sweet smelling and attractive, cocoa hulls are an excellent mulch for landscapes close to people. They are more expensive than other mulches, though, which makes them primarily applicable to small areas. They are also somewhat poor at weed suppression. They may turn white with fungus if kept moist, but the material is good for the soil and poses no threat to people nor, generally speaking, to pets. Hulls are quick to decompose and release small amounts of nitrogen, phosphate and potassium. Cocoa hulls can be lethal to pets that eat a lot of woody mulch.

Gorilla Hair: Attractive and long lasting, gorilla hair is a mulch made from redwood shaved into thin long fibrous strands. It is fantastic as a walking surface. Gorilla hair has some drawbacks, however: it soaks up a lot of water, meaning less makes it into the soil; it is easily blown around a property; it is not a good weed suppressant because of its airy nature; and it is a very ignitable material. It will initially rob nitrogen and when completely decomposed it will provide a little nitrogen, phosphorus and potassium. Gorilla hair should not be used in fire hazard areas.

Grass Clippings: Because they contain moderate amounts of nitrogen, grass clippings should always be given back to a landscape. However, directly laying them down over the soil is not an effective way to do this. If the clippings are dry, then they will break down in the sun and blow about the property. If kept moist, they will create an acidic barrier on top of the soil. Both situations will cause nitrogen to be released into the atmosphere instead of the soil. Grass clippings should be composted and the nutrients returned as mulch.

Humus: Humus is finely decomposed organic matter that is nutrient rich. It is acidic and helps acidify soils. It is an excellent remedy for alkaline soils and the iron deficiencies that are a consequence. It is vital to organic food production. The amount of available nutrients in humus depends on the materials that were used to create it. Humus is not good at weed suppression.

Humus is called Back Gold by gardeners. It is finely decomposed organic matter, nutrient rich and slightly acidic. Most California Friendly plants require little more than humus for fertilization.

Leaves: Leaves have many benefits. They are probably the most abundant mulching material in urban areas. They have more nutrients than woody material. They are generally quick to decompose (though there are some exceptions, such as oak leaves). And they can be effective at weed suppression. Leaves high in oils (such as camphor, eucalyptus, juniper, and pine) are the best for weed suppression. A thick layer of broadleaf leaves in damp conditions can create an acidic barrier and prevent a soil from exchanging gases, ultimately undermining plant health.

Manure: Spreading manure over the top of soil is a practice thousands of years old. Manures can be rich in nutrients, readily decompose, and help improve the tilth of soil. However, as a mulch, manures are not the best. Their salts can damage plants; their odors offend neighbors, and they are not good at weed suppression. In urban areas manures are worked into the soil to improve its levels of microscopic life and nutrients.

Sawdust: Sawdust can be an attractive mulch, but it makes a better soil amendment because it tends to blow around a landscape. Fungus will develop on sawdust in damp conditions. It is not effective for weed suppression. Sawdust will initially rob the soil of nitrogen and when completely decomposed it will have contributed a little nitrogen, phosphorus and potassium.

Straw: Bright colored and attractive, straw is a good mulch around food crops because it does not hold moisture and will not cause rot. While straw will initially rob nitrogen, it does contribute beneficial amounts of potassium when decomposed. Straw is not so good at weed suppression. Straw should not be used in fire hazard areas.

Tree Chippings / Shredding: One of the least expensive mulches and the best for weed suppression, this material comes from tree service companies and is produced by chipping recently pruned vegetation. It will initially rob nitrogen and the amount of nutrients it returns depends on the amount of leaves in the chippings; the more leaves, the more nutrients.

Quick Tips for Applying Mulch

Amount: To get all the benefits of organic mulches (water conservation, weed suppression, etc.) no less that a 2" layer is needed; anything more than 4" is redundant. If a plant is prone to rot, keep mulches several inches away from its crown. Killing (smothering) the weeds already growing in an area requires a 6" layer of mulch.

Timing: Deterring mulches are generally needed no more than once a year. The best time to apply them is early winter, or just before weeds start taking off. Nourishing mulches may be needed twice a year. The best times are early spring, when plants need a blast of nutrients, and early fall, when the soil needs protection from rain and runoff.

Supplemental Nitrogen: If coarse woody mulches are used around nutrient-needy plants, it will be necessary to provide supplemental nitrogen because deterring mulches initially rob the soil of nitrogen. The added nitrogen will not only help maintain plant health, but also speed the decomposition of the mulch. Blood meal and fishmeal are excellent supplements. If nourishing mulches are used, such as compost, then nitrogen supplements are generally not needed.

Overcoming Compacted Soils

Compaction is the norm for urban soils. Too much water and too much traffic leads to compaction, and that leads to a soil's inability to exchange its gases, which in turn leads to lower levels of oxygen, acidic conditions and a landscape that is quick to produce runoff. All of these issues undermine the goals of plant health and resource conservation. Below are recommendations for overcoming compaction.

■ Keep Some Weeds. The plants that colonize compacted soils are specialized early succession pioneers; they help prepare the area for the later successions by loosening and enriching the soil.

■ Cycles of Dry and Wet: Letting a soil become bone-dry, saturating it, and then letting it completely dry again will physically break the bonds of compaction. Dense soils are expansive and will visibly rise and fall with this type of water schedule, eventually reducing compaction.

■ Redirect Traffic: Directing traffic away from an area will help alleviate the source of compaction.

■ Mulch: Laying a thick layer of woody mulch will help reduce compaction by distributing the weight of traffic.

■ Aerate: Aeration, whether done by hand or by machine, is a quick and effective way to restore permeability. One or two inches of fine mulch or compost should be raked into an area after aeration.

■ Cover Crop. Planting cover crops is an excellent way to break up compacted soils and load them with vital nutrients. Also known as green manures, cover crops are comprised of grasses, such as barley and oats, and annuals in the pea family, such as beans, clover, and vetch.

■ Turning Soil Mechanically: Turning over the soil through brute force will absolutely reduce compaction. Whether by hand or a machine, organic material should be added to the turning process to help avoid compaction recurring again.

Maintaining Grade: Dry Landscapes Should Dip

Mounding garden beds are holdovers from a time when water was more plentiful in Southern California. We built up landscapes to help ensure plant health and improve aesthetics. But the health and aesthetics came at a cost. These elevated areas need more irrigation and are less capable of capturing rainfall and snowmelt. We can no longer afford to irrigate more and capture less. Southern Californians need to dip, rather than mound, their landscapes.

California Friendly landscapes sit below impermeable surfaces, such as driveways, parking lots and sidewalks. Any water that falls on a landscape will naturally flow to the plants, instead of pooling or running away. Below are the general characteristics of dipping the grade of a landscape.

Depth: Landscaped areas should sit no less than 1" below impermeable surfaces; 2" is better. Maintaining this grade will entail re-grading every 4 to 8 years. The buildup of soil with either have to be moved somewhere else on the property or hauled away.

Compaction: As soils go down, compaction goes up. The lowest areas of a landscape may need protection from water pooling, trampling and compaction. Shrubs and aggressive ground covers will help protect the soil and prevent compaction.

Irrigation: Lower lying areas need less irrigation than mounded areas; where a mound might require irrigation twice a week, a low area only once. Always let the soil dry to the plants' dry-to-depth, as discussed in the Irrigation and Plant chapters.

When this community was originally built the soil was below the grade of the structures. No longer. In a heavy rain this bugling landscape will shed water instead of absorbing it, endangering the homes, walkways and public safety.

14

Rainwater Capture: Rain Barrels and Cisterns

Rainwater harvesting is simply capturing water and storing it for future use. It's an impulse as natural as tilting back your head and opening your mouth to catch a taste of a late-spring rain. It is an art and practice thousands of years old.

Nothing beats rainwater for purity. Rain starts with zero bacteria, chemicals and salt. Only the air it falls through and the surfaces it runs off contaminate it. Rain is incredibly soft (no minerals) and slightly acidic. For these reasons, plants prefer rainwater above all other water sources.

Despite these fantastic benefits, rainwater capture can become a public nuisance if not properly maintained. It can inadvertently create vector problems by increasing the population of insects and animals that transmit disease to humans. It can leak or malfunction, which can cause pooling, runoff and rot problems to the site's infrastructure. A long-term commitment to maintenance will ensure all of rainwater's the benefits without any of the above-mentioned the risks to public health and urban infrastructure.

Arlington Garden, Pasadena.

Maintenance

The basic steps of rainwater harvesting are capture, transport, screening, storage, and distribution. Rainwater falls on a roof, is channeled into gutters, screened of large debris, transported to a storage device, and then finally delivered to the landscape either by gravity or a pump. The drawing below illustrates these steps. Following it is a description of the maintenance required at each point.

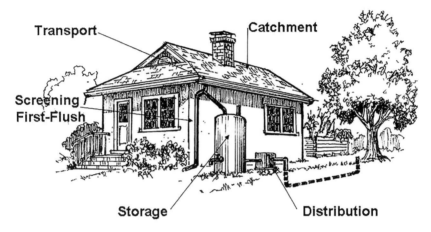

Drawing by Richard Kent

Rainwater Capture Surface: The Roof

Any surface that allows water to sheet and run can be used to capture rain. Naturally, the cleaner the surface, the cleaner the water and the longer it can be stored without significant change to its quality. Maintaining a clean surface ensures better water quality. Sweeping or blowing the debris off the roof and gutters helps ensure better quality.

Avoid Collecting Water from Toxic Surfaces

The water that runs off some surfaces should not be collected and stored—it might create a toxic soup. The surfaces to avoid include:

■ Petroleum-based surfaces, such a asphalt, slurry and tar.

■ Surfaces treated with a preservative, such as wood shingles.

■ Rough surfaces (They trap more particulates and dust and are more likely to support algae, bacteria, mold and moss).

The fact that these surfaces produce water too toxic for storage means that the water is also damaging to our rivers, lakes and ocean. Rainwater coming off contaminated surfaces should be led to the landscape where the toxins can be naturally changed or removed.

This is not an ideal situation for rainwater capture. Under several *Eucalyptuses* that shed profusely water collected from this roof will be full of leaves and spoil quickly.

Transport System

To get rainwater from a surface to a storage device requires a system of transport. Gutters do this job. The single most important part of maintaining the efficient transport of rainwater is keeping gutters clean. From misdirected and spilling water, to pooling and mosquito problems, cleanliness affects the quality and quantity of water collected.

- Clean the leaf guards before every major storm to ensure proper flow.

- Repair damage to gutters to reduce leaking and pooling.

- Maintain a proper slope. Gutters must have a slight incline to efficiently move water. No less that a ¼" fall per 10 feet is required, and a ½" fall is recommended.

- Replace interlocking gutters with continuous gutters to greatly reduce opportunities for leaks, spills and pooling.

Diversion and Screening Devices

After months without rain a roof will be exceptionally dirty. This water must either be finely screened or diverted away from a storage container. There are inexpensive techniques, such as manually directing a downspout to a landscape, installing funnels with filters, and making first-flush boxes. Expensive systems will have pumps, extensive filters and electronically regulated diversion systems.

After the initial cleaning, all subsequent work will be aimed at screening organic debris, such as feathers and leaves, from being swept into storage. Screening is essential because the cleaner the water coming into storage, the cleaner it will be when is comes out, and the cleaner the water, the more uses it has. Screening devices are fairly inexpensive and include gutter screens, leaf-guards and strainers.

Gutter screens should be cleaned before the start of every storm.

Not only will this fine-mesh screen prevent debris from getting into the rain barrel, but also mosquitos.

Storage: Barrels and Cisterns

Capturing rain is easy; storing it properly can be a challenge. Algae, pooling, mosquitos and misdirected water are common problems with poorly maintained storage systems. Storing rainwater is not a low maintenance practice. Below are the essentials of maintaining a healthy and effective storage system.

Benefits of Elevating the Barrels

The higher off the ground the stored water is the greater its energy potential and the greater its use. Increasing water pressure and rates of flow also makes cleaning the barrels easier.

Height of Barrel	Water Pressure (psi)	Useful Distance of Hose
On Ground		
Full	1.30	18'
Nearly Empty	0.00	0
2' Off Ground		
Full	2.16	30'
Nearly Empty	0.866	12'
4' Off Ground		
Full	3.03	42'
Nearly Empty	1.73	24'
6' Off Ground		
Full	3.90	54'
Nearly Empty	2.60	36'

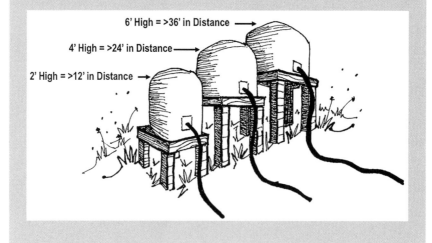

6' High = >36' in Distance

4' High = >24' in Distance

2' High = >12' in Distance

Inspection: Before the start of the rainy season inspect the barrel or cistern, looking for cracks, loose fittings, a tears in screens, and joints that might need a fresh application of plumber's grease or silicon.

Cleaning: Rain barrels should be emptied out and cleaned of algae and sediment no less that once a year. If algae is a problem, scrub the inside with a solution of either vinegar and water (1 gallon per 1 gallon), bleach and water (¾ cup per 1 gallon), or hydrogen peroxide and water (1.5 cups per 1 gallon). Be sure to dispose of the vinegar, bleach or hydrogen peroxide in the sewer system—not a landscape or storm drain!

Painting: Many people paint their barrels/cisterns, either to reflect sunlight or to match the color of a structure. Cooling a container with paint is effective and can increase the longevity of the entire system. Plastic storage units will need painting every 2 to 3 years.

The Essentials of Maintenance

The maintenance of rainwater harvesting systems falls into three categories: cleaning, protecting and replacing.

Cleaning: Cleaning is an essential and ongoing task. Starting from the catchment area and working towards the eventual outfall, every screen, filter and catch basin must be cleaned prior to the rainy season every year. Every other year the debris at the bottom of storage devices should be removed.

Protecting: A rainwater harvest system needs protection from the environment. Heat, cold and animals all cause a lot of damage. A system will last longer in the shade and steady temperatures; the north side of structures is the best location. Shading devices, such as cloth and structures, as well as light reflecting paint, will also increase the longevity of the system. Protecting the plumbing and storage tank from freezing will decrease chances of ruptures and fissures. This may require insulation for the pipes and placing a water heater in the tank. Make sure there are no access points for insects and animals by fixing all leaks, and repairing and replacing barriers.

Replacing: Maintenance means replacing fittings and filters, gutters and downspouts. Depending on exposure and use, most, if not all, of a rain storage system will have to be replaced in 20 years. This means that ¹⁄₂₀th of the initial cost must be paid out (or saved) for the system every year. Maintenance means doing a little at a time, all the time.

Thwarting Mosquitoes

Creating anxiety and discomfort, inflicting bites and disease, mosquitoes ruin a favorite Southern California ritual—enjoying the sunset at dusk. Storing water on a property increases the chances of mosquitoes. To safely store water and continue to enjoy the sunset follow the maintenance recommendations listed below:

Bti (*Bacillus thuringiensis israelensis*): A larvicide that is used in water with access to the atmosphere. *Bti* is a bacterium that is toxic to the larvae of mosquitoes as well as some blackflies and gnats. It is available at any home improvement store and not much is needed for a 55-gallon barrel. Since *Bti* does not work on the other 3 stages of a mosquito, it must be combined with other strategies.

Draining Barrels: Draining a barrel once a week is very effective because mosquitoes go from egg to adult in 7 to 10 days. Be sure to remove any water that pools in top of the storage device.

Drain Rock: Water tends to pool around rain barrels. Placing barrels on a 6" layer of crushed drain rock will alleviate this surface pooling.

Securing Fittings: Make sure that the lid, vents and all incoming and outgoing pipes are properly secured. For systems that are regularly used and/or jostled, replacing gaskets and resealing fittings with silicon can be a yearly task.

Mosquitofish (*Gambusia affinis*): One mosquitofish can eat 300 mosquito larvae a day. Open-air storage devices, like troughs, benefit the most from these fish. The major drawback with mosquitofish is that people get attached to them and are reluctant to drain the troughs and which kills the fish. Mosquitofish are free in Southern California. Simply call your local Vector Control District to get a supply. Mosquitofish are not necessarily appropriate for rain barrels. They need just the right amount of water, temperature and light, and rain barrels rarely provide the right combination of these three needs. Exclusion and source reduction are the best options for barrels.

Screens: Any opening to the stored water that cannot be securely closed requires a mosquito screen. Mesh no larger than 1/16" is needed to adequately screen overflow pipes and lid openings. Window screen mesh is an inexpensive and effective option.

Mosquitoes go through their life cycle fairly quickly. They have 4 stages: egg, larvae, pupae and adult. The first 3 take place in the water and take only 7 to 10 days to complete. Adults may live a couple of months. Only females bite; they need the blood for their eggs. The buzzing you hear is related to mating.

PART VI

Additional Resources

Resources

Los Angeles Department of Water and Power (LADWP)

LADWP is the nation's largest municipal utility. They have provided water and power services to Los Angeles residents for over 100 years. LADWP offers numerous rebates and programs to help their customers save water and money.

Water Conservation: www.ladwp.com/wc.

In this site are all the resources needed for commercial and residential property managers to save water both indoor and out. This site includes information on rebates, training seminars, and water conservation ordinances and codes.

California Friendly® Landscaping: www.ladwp.cafriendlylandscaping.com.

LADWP explains how to design and install California Friendly® Landscape. This site also provides comprehensive tips for maintaining irrigation efficiency and gives suggestions on successfully maintaining your garden.

Metropolitan Water District of Southern California (MWD)

MWD is the largest distributor of treated drinking water in the United States. It is a wholesaler that delivers water to 26 member public agencies, which in turn provides water to more than 19 million people in Los Angeles, Orange, Riverside, San Bernardino, San Diego and Ventura counties. MWD provides an array of resources for commercial and residential water conservation.

BeWaterWise.com: www.bewaterwise.com

This site has links to water conservation rebates, innovation grants, and extensive tips and suggestions, including a complete guide to California Friendly® landscaping.

Home and Garden: www.bewaterwise.com/gardenspot

This site provides information on classes for landscape design, irrigation and maintenance, landscape rebates, and a complete design and plant guide for commercial and residential landscapes

Southern California Gas Company (SoCalGas)

SoCalGas is the nation's largest natural gas distribution utility and safely serves more than 21 million consumers through nearly 5.9 million meters in more than 500 communities. SoCalGas offers many of resources for customers to save energy, water and money.

Energy Upgrade California® Home Upgrade:

www.socalgas.com/save-money-and-energy/rebates-and-incentives/energy-upgrade-california

The Home Upgrade program can help make your home more comfortable, improve air quality, help you save energy and possibly lower your energy bills.

Energy Resource Center:

www.socalgas.com/for-your-business/education-and-training/energy-resource-center

The SoCalGas Energy Resource Center (ERC) is an energy-efficiency partner for energy and environmental decision makers. The facility is dedicated to sustainability and achieved LEED Existing Building Operations and Maintenance (version 4) Platinum Certification in June of 2015. The ERC offers seminars, demonstrations and consulting services to help businesses find cost-effective, energy-efficient solutions. They also host a beautiful California Friendly® demonstration garden.

Buried utilities can exist just about anywhere on a property – it is essential to check with DigAlert before digging. You can prevent damage to underground utilities and avoid service interruptions simply by utilizing our online service   DigAlert Express or calling 811 two (2) business days prior to starting your excavation. This is a 100% free service, and more importantly – it is the law.

DigAlert must be consulted at least two day prior to digging. Some of the common reasons why gardeners, landscapers and contractors call DigAlert include digging for irrigation, planting trees and shrubs, installing fence posts, building ponds, and installing a mailbox.

©2017 Underground Service Alert of Southern California.

Index